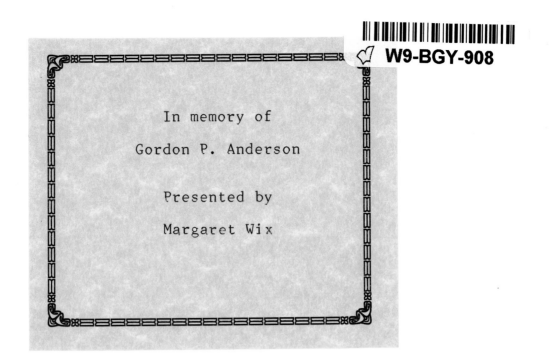

ENCYCLOPEDIA OF
WOODWORKING

ENCYCLOPEDIA OF
WOODWORKING

The complete guide to materials, tools and techniques
20 step-by-step projects

ALAN AND GILL BRIDGEWATER

NEW
HOLLAND

First published in 2007 by New Holland Publishers (UK) Ltd

London • Cape Town • Sydney • Auckland

Garfield House, 86–88 Edgware Road, London W2 2EA, United Kingdom

www.newhollandpublishers.com

80 McKenzie Street, Cape Town 8001, South Africa

Unit 1, 66 Gibbes Street, Chatswood, NSW 2067, Australia

218 Lake Road, Northcote, Auckland

ISBN 978 184537 6772

1 3 5 7 9 10 8 6 4 2

Editorial Direction: Rosemary Wilkinson

Senior Editor: Caroline Blake

Production: Hazel Kirkman

Designed and created for New Holland by AG&G Books

Design: Glyn Bridgewater

Woodwork: Chris and Don Waring of SCJ

Illustrations: Coral Mula

Editor: Fiona Corbridge

Photographs: AG&G Books

Reproduction by Modern Age Repro, Hong Kong

Printed and bound in Malaysia by Times Offset (M) Sdn. Bhd.

The information in this book is true and complete to the best of our knowledge. All recommendations are made without guarantee on the part of the authors and the publishers. The authors and publishers disclaim any liability for damages or injury resulting from the use of this information.

ACKNOWLEDGMENTS

A special thanks to **Chris** and **Don Waring** of **SCJ** for their excellent woodwork, ju-jitsu and jokes. Thanks also to Jill Lewis who let us photograph the bench in her beautiful garden (page 134). AG&G Books and New Holland Publishers would also like to thank the following makers who kindly supplied photographs of their work:
Alexander Brady <www.alexanderbrady.co.uk>,
Bruce Burman <www.burmanfinefurniture.co.uk>, **Paul Dean** <www.artmarquetry.com>,
Bob Dillon <www.bobdillonwindsorchairs.com>,
Ronnie Graham <www.irishbogwoodsculpture.com>,
Kevin Neelley <www.turnedwood.com>, **Raymond Lanham** <www.woodcentral.com>, **Erve Moninger** <marjie@bytehead.com>, **Chris Pye** <www.chrispye-woodcarving.com> and **David Savage** <www.finefurnituremaker.com>.
The following suppliers kindly provided photographs of their products:
Anita Marquetry Ltd, **Axminster Power Tool Centre** and **Screwfix Direct Ltd**.

CONTENTS

INTRODUCTION

Wood is probably the most versatile of all materials; it is easily cut and shaped, incredibly strong and available in hundreds of colours, textures and grain patterns. Each piece of wood is unique and its surface appears different each time it is cut. It is available as massive sections of tree trunk, sawn planks of various sizes, small, precious pieces for woodturning, and as thin sheets of decorative veneer. Everyone seems to like the warm, rich, "natural" texture of wood. Who can resist sliding their hands over the surface of a polished oak tabletop or stroking the worn-away, burnished arm of a Windsor chair?

*Sideboard in English oak with bog oak detailing, oil
and wax polished, by designer and maker Bruce Burman.*

Working with wood can be very satisfying. Removing fine shavings with a smoothing plane, scooping out hollows with a gouge, steam-bending bow shapes, cutting perfect joints and achieving a fine finish are pleasures not to be missed.

A bird carved from bog oak by Ronnie Graham.

Making your own furniture can save you money and the quality of your own woodwork will surpass anything that you can buy in a superstore. There is also the thought that your great-great-grandchildren will sit in your chair and admire your workmanship!

Woodworking is not really a "kitchen-table" craft (generally you do need a whole room, shed or outdoor space in which to work), but it does not need to be physically demanding or expensive. Power tools are getting cheaper all the time and it is amazing what you can make with just a jigsaw and a router. Buy prepared timber if space is limited, or if you do not want to handle large pieces of timber or invest in large pieces of machinery. On the other hand, if you enjoy buying tools and machines, there is a tantalizing array of options.

This book explains the basic techniques required for successful woodworking, introduces specialized subjects such as turning, marquetry, steam-bending and carving, and presents twenty specially commissioned woodworking projects with step-by-step instructions. In addition, numerous samples of wood species and examples of other people's work provide further reference and inspiration.

A turned bowl made from contrasting woods by Kevin Neelley.

WOOD 1

TREES

No two pieces of wood – even from the same tree – are exactly the same. The best way to enjoy your woodworking journey is to have a clear understanding of wood's possibilities. If you know about colour, texture and working characteristics, you are three-quarters of the way there.

HARDWOODS AND SOFTWOODS

Hardwood comes from broad-leafed deciduous trees that drop their leaves annually, and softwood comes from coniferous, cone-bearing evergreens that retain their foliage (but there are exceptions). Hardwood is generally harder in texture, harder to work, more dense in structure, heavier, stronger and more durable than softwood (but again, there are exceptions). For example, cedar is a softwood (soft in texture, light in weight) but is more durable than many hardwoods; and lime (basswood) is a hardwood but is soft in texture and easy to work. And, while a hardwood such as European oak is durable, American red oak is not.

Softwood normally grows quickly; it is cheap, available as narrow planks (from small trunks) with many knots, and is used for paper-making, house-building and low-cost furniture. Hardwood tends to take a long time to grow; it is expensive, available in wide boards (from large trunks) with few knots, and is used for furniture-making.

Softwood furniture tends to be chunkier than hardwood furniture as bulkier sections are required in order to achieve the same structural strength. Softwood tends to expand and contract – "move", twist and warp – more readily than hardwood.

A newly planted forest of beech trees.

Softwood trees in a young forest.

Beech "coppice" woodland (the tree is cut at ground level to produce multiple shoots that grow into poles).

GRAIN AND GROWTH

The grain, or patterns and textures, that we see in a length of planed wood is directly related to the growth of the tree. Many characteristics of grain are inherent to species – straight-grained lime, coarse- and wavy-grained European oak – but grain is also affected by growth. For example, slow and even growth results in a close grain, fast growth in a coarse grain, and irregular growth in cross-grain and badly aligned grain.

A slice through a tree will reveal loosely packed sapwood at the outer edges, and densely packed heartwood at the centre, with good and bad growing years being shown by wide or narrow annual rings. Generally, the central heartwood of slow-grown timber, with its compacted rings and full colour, is considered to be the best wood.

WHICH PARTS OF A TREE ARE USED?

Traditionally, every last bit of a tree was used, from the base through to the bark and branches. Nowadays, the most commercially usable boards come from the trunk or butt, meaning the straight length of tree that runs from the ground up to where the boughs and large limbs fork off. This part renders the most consistent sections, which are especially desirable for furniture-making.

Large limbs, boughs and crotches produce very useful and visually exciting sections for woodturning, carving, veneering, boat-building, house construction and so on. Some of the most beautiful and prized wood is obtained from the buttress, burrs, crotches and knots.

The end of an English oak butt (base of the trunk) clearly shows the annual rings. Checking (splits) occurs in whole trunks that are allowed to dry (season) before they are sawn into planks.

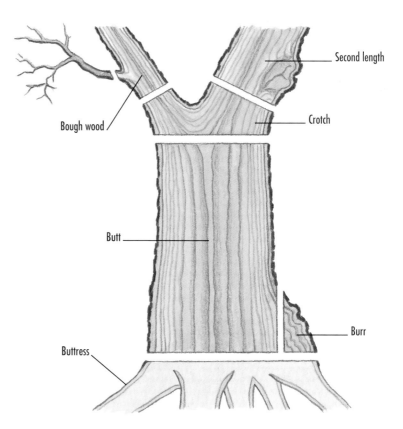

Second length

Bough wood

Crotch

Butt

Burr

Buttress

A cross-section through a typical hardwood tree showing the various portions that are used for woodworking projects.

SOLID WOOD

Selecting solid wood is exciting, but you have to avoid making expensive mistakes, such as choosing the wrong type of wood, or poor-quality wood. The best way of ensuring that you finish up with wood that is "fitting for its purpose", is to know something about conversion, seasoning, grain and faults.

CONVERSION

The size, shape and grain pattern of timber, as purchased from a supplier, is determined by the way the tree is sawn, or converted. There are many traditional ways of converting a tree. It can be plain sawn to make a stack of planks, radial or quarter sawn, modularly sawn, and so on. The converting method, and the resultant angle at which the growth rings within the tree meet the sawn face, are the factors that shape the grain pattern or figure that is seen on the surface of the finished timber.

SEASONING

Seasoning is the controlled drying of the sawn wood. There are two methods – the wood can be carefully stacked and air-dried (every inch of thickness takes

This valuable stock of yew will probably be bought by a specialist sawmill, converted into narrow planks and sold to furniture-makers or other craftspeople.

Taking full advantage of the flexibility of wet, unseasoned ("green") coppice wood.

These oak boards are ready to use. Each layer is separated by sticks to allow air to circulate.

about a year to dry), or it can be dried in a kiln in about six months. The stability, strength and overall colour and character of finished, ready-to-use timber hinges on two factors: the way it is converted and the speed of seasoning. If it is done correctly, the wood will be stable and well coloured; if it is not, the wood will be variously split, bowed and otherwise less than perfect.

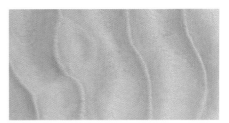

Swept grain in American walnut.

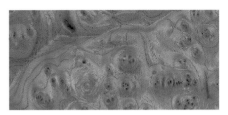

Quilted maple.

Medullary rays in brown oak.

Burr elm.

GRAIN AND FIGURE

The term "grain" refers to the direction of fibres as they occur naturally within a tree, and "figure" is the overall arrangement of grain and colour within cut wood. But both terms are used loosely to describe the colour and pattern seen on the surface of wood. The precise character of the figure is decided by the way the wood is converted. Straight grain is the most common type.

BUYING WOOD

Nowadays it is difficult to buy small quantities of wood for fine woodworking projects because small, local sawmills are going out of business. They cannot compete with large timber importers. The result is that you will probably have to travel a long way to get to a timberyard, the stock is unlikely to include home-grown species, and their boards will be kiln-dried, straight-grained and a bit bland. For unseasoned wood, waney-edged planks and exciting grain patterns, try one of the specialist timber suppliers listed at the back of the book, or look at the advertisements in a woodworking magazine.

Kiln-dried, imported timber stored in a warehouse.

FAULTS TO AVOID

- **Bowing and winding** – Diagonal twists in a board.
- **Cupping** – A board that is bowed across its width.

- **Cup checks** – Splits that occur towards the middle of a tree.
- **Decay** – Shows as rot, mould and unusual stains.
- **Encased knots** – Remains of branches that show as large, bark-filled knots.
- **Heart checks** – A cavity at the heart of the wood.
- **Insect attack** – Holes that show that a pest has entered, eaten and exited.
- **Loose knots** – Unsound knots that indicate decay.

- **Round checks** – Loose rings at the heart of a tree, which suggest that the tree was old and/or stressed.
- **Through checks** – A split that runs from one face to another.
- **Splits** – General splits caused by poor seasoning.
- **Springing** – Movement in a board, which shows as a bowed edge – caused by poor seasoning.
- **Waney edges** – An edge on a prepared board that shows unusable bark.

13

A TO Z OF WOODS

Trees vary in size, colour and character – one species will only yield short, narrow boards; another will yield giant boards. Some wood is bland in colour and texture; some is a brilliant colour with a wild texture. One of the secrets of good woodwork is to select wood that is perfect for your needs.

CHOOSING WOODS

Satellite photography clearly shows us that the destruction of the Earth's forests has not abated; the Amazon rainforest, for example, is shrinking twice as fast as previously thought.

Perhaps now is the time to be eco-selective when choosing wood from the thousands of tree species. Consider your needs – colour, character, texture and size – and then make a careful choice. If you know that a wood is rare, listed, endangered or no longer commercially available, think about using a more planet-friendly alternative. Or perhaps you could use a common wood for the main structure and cover it with a thin veneer of precious wood. While a wood such as Brazilian rosewood is altogether beautiful and desirable, it is both endangered and banned. Of course you might still be able to obtain and use such a wood, but most reputable makers, designers and specialists would, at the very least, be saddened to see an item made of it.

The good news is that there are hundreds of wonderful non-endangered species out there. A good way forward is to study our list, look at pieces of furniture in shows and suchlike, and then search out a reputable local supplier. The best option of all is to hunt out a good local sawmill – one that converts and seasons its own local timber – and use that. Also, there is no reason why you cannot use recycled wood, such as old furniture, old floorboards or whatever comes your way.

This sideboard, by designer and maker Bruce Burman, combines a variety of woods in an elegant design that showcases his craftsmanship.

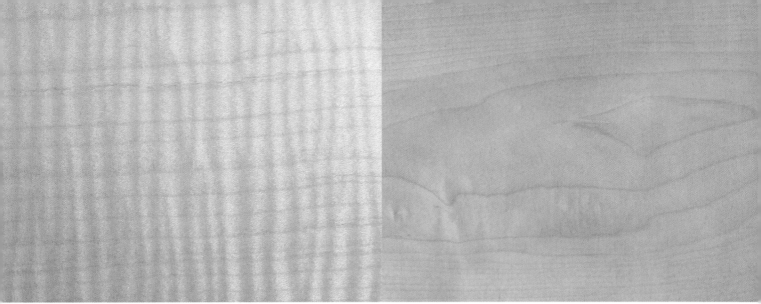

FIDDLEBACK SYCAMORE
Acer pseudoplatanus Sycamore plane, Great maple

Sycamore is a medium-textured, straight-grained hardwood. Colour: white. Fiddleback sycamore (illustrated) has a beautiful rippled texture and is traditionally used for violin backs. Sycamore dyes better than any other wood and can be purchased as colourful veneers or inlays.

AMERICAN MAPLE
Acer rubrum Canadian maple, Soft maple

A hard-textured, straight-grained hardwood. Colour: cream. Not as strong as rock maple, but much the same in overall character. Very good for furniture and woodturning – can be worked to a fine, crisp-edged finish.

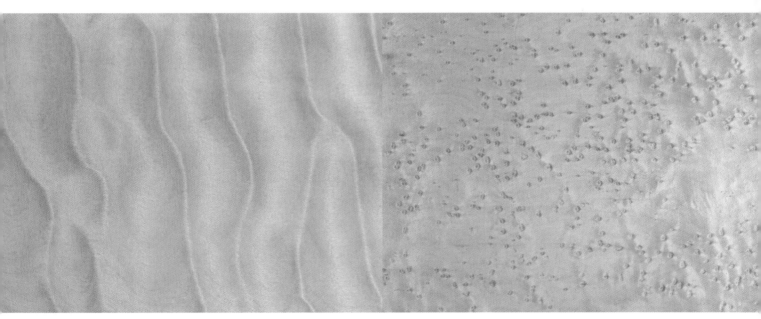

QUILTED MAPLE
Acer saccharum Clouded maple, Guitar maple

A hard-textured, close-grained hardwood. Colour: cream-brown to golden brown. The photograph shows a quilted figure, one of the rarest grain patterns known. The figure can be supplied in burr or burl and in timber sections. Veneers taken from the burr are used almost exclusively for decorating guitars. Quilted maple was very popular in the 1930s, when it was used to decorate Art Deco furniture.

HARD MAPLE
Acer saccharum Rock maple

A hard-textured, close-grained hardwood. Colour: cream-brown to golden brown. The photograph shows bird's-eye maple, which isn't in itself a variety or species of maple, but rather a phenomenon that occurs within the tree. The swirling grain of bird's-eye maple makes it a choice option for woodturning and use as a veneer.

PARANA PINE
Araucaria angustifolia **Brazilian pine**

A smooth-textured, straight-grained softwood. Colour: cream to honey; red to pink. Very smooth and easy to work – good for interior joinery, furniture, toys and small turned items. It can be used anywhere where there is a need for long, knot-free boards, such as on doors, staircases and tabletops.

BURR MADRONNA
Arbutus menziesii **Madrono**

A straight-grained hardwood. Colour: cream to brown; red to brown. Available in large board widths. A very difficult wood to work. The photograph shows a burr. The swirling grain makes it a great choice for use as a veneer, or for woodturning.

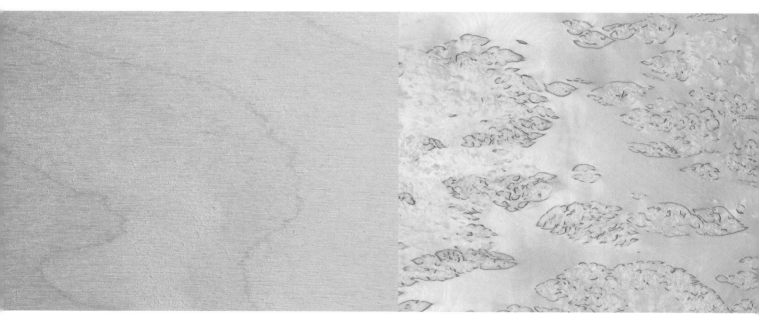

PAPER BIRCH
Betula papyrifera

Medium-textured, straight-grained hardwood. Colour: white to pale brown. Mainly used for high-quality plywood, but is also used in modern furniture and decorative turnings. Sometimes displays a curly grain pattern known as "flame birch".

MASSUR (EUROPEAN) BIRCH
Betula pendula **Swedish birch**

"Massur" birch is the term for a freak pattern in birch. The parent tree is a fine-textured, straight-grained hardwood. Colour: cream to pale brown. The characteristic dappled and dotted patterns are much the same colour, but covered in a pattern of holes that look as though they have been pecked. A good choice for woodturning and decorative veneers.

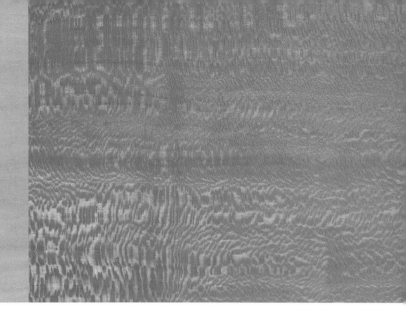

BOXWOOD
Buxus sempervirens **English box, American box**
A very hard, dense-grained hardwood. Colour: pale yellow-cream. Only available in very narrow board widths. Box is the perfect choice for small items such as boxes, turned knobs and miniature carvings. It was traditionally used by wood engravers. It is difficult to work, but it can be brought to a crisp, shiny finish.

LACEWOOD
Cardwellia sublimis **Silky oak, Australian oak**
A coarse-textured, straight-grained hardwood. Colour: pink to red. Rather like a piece of straight-grained American oak. A choice option for exterior work, furniture-making and general interior work. Reasonably priced if you live in Australia, but a bit expensive if you live in America or Europe.

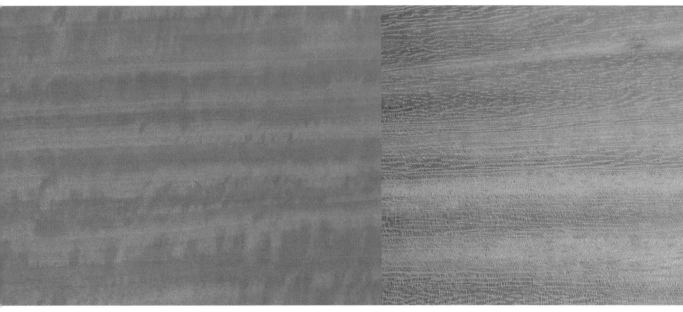

CEYLON SATINWOOD
Chloroxylon swietenia **East Indian satinwood**
A fine-textured, wavy-grained hardwood. Colour: gold to yellow; brown to orange. A good choice for furniture-making, woodturning and general interior joinery. The wood is heavy, hard and strong. It is difficult to work; nevertheless, with a lot of effort and sharp tools, the surface can be brought to a high-shine finish.

IROKO
Clorophora excelsa
A medium-textured, irregular-grained hardwood. Colour: red-brown. Very durable. Used most frequently for outdoor furniture as a cheaper alternative to teak; also for joinery and parquet flooring, and for carving and turning.

MEXICAN ROSEWOOD
Dalbergia retusa Honduras rosewood

Sometimes mistakenly called Brazilian rosewood (*Dalbergia nigra*), this is a coarse-textured, straight- to wavy-grained hardwood. Colour: gold to brown; purple to chocolate. Produces medium to large board widths. Expensive, so used primarily for small work – woodturning, carving, and decorative veneers. This is an endangered species: make sure that you get your wood from a reputable supplier.

MACASSAR EBONY
Diospyros celebica East Indian ebony, Golden ebony

A dense, straight- to wavy-grained hardwood. Colour: brown to black, striped hardwood. It looks, depending upon the width of the stripes, either black with brown stripes, or brown with black stripes. A durable wood, but very difficult to work. Good for small items such as carved miniatures and small boxes, veneering and woodturning. It is both rare and expensive.

JELUTONG
Dyera costulata Chewing gum tree

A lightweight, bland-textured, straight-grained hardwood. Colour: yellow to white; gold to yellow. Jelutong is very easy to work – not as soft as balsa wood, but much the same in general appearance. Looks best when it's painted. More than anything else, jelutong is used for low-cost woodcarving. It's a great choice for beginners.

SAPELE
Entandrophragma cylindricum Aboudikro

A fine-textured, straight-grained hardwood. Colour: cream to yellow; pink to brown. It was overused as a decorative finish during the 1960s and 1970s, when it was popular for flush doors and interiors, so it is now thought of as rather passé. However, it is still a good wood.

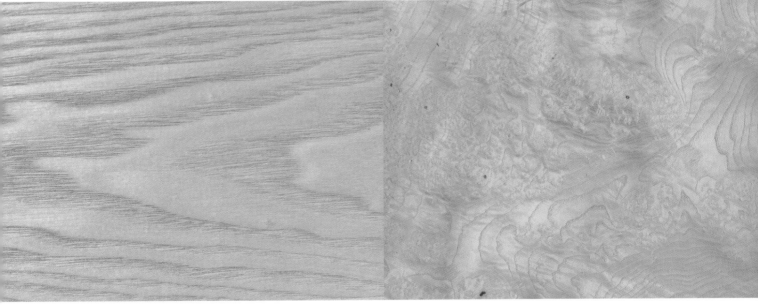

UTILE
Entandrophragma utile Afau-konkonti, Kosi-kosi, Sipo

A dense, irregular-grained hardwood. Colour: red-brown. Commonly used for furniture, joinery and shop-fitting. Can be brought to a high finish once the grain has been filled.

AMERICAN BEECH
Fagus grandifolia

A heavy, strong, straight-grained hardwood. Colour: yellow-brown sapwood and red to brown heartwood. Great for furniture, toys, woodturning and suchlike. A good option for hand tool work. It can be worked to a beautiful, crisp-edged finish. Apart from being a bit more rugged to the touch, it has more or less the same working characteristics as European beech (*Fagus sylvatica*).

AMERICAN ASH
Fraxinus americana White ash

A very tough, long-grained hardwood. Colour: pale pinkish brown to pale white-brown. A good choice for steam-bending, tool handles, chair legs and turning. Although it is very difficult to work, it can be brought to a very attractive, smooth finish. Produces medium to narrow boards. The American and European varieties have more or less the same characteristics.

BURR ASH
Fraxinus excelsior European burl ash

A burr is a warty growth on a tree. In this instance, the burr or burl has all the characteristics of the parent ash – a tough, long-grained hardwood. As with most burrs, it is that much more difficult to work. Colour: red-brown to pale white-brown. A good choice for small woodturnings, and for decorative veneers. Burr or burl veneers tend to be extremely brittle.

SILKY OAK
Grevillea robusta Australian silky oak

A coarse-textured, straight-grained hardwood. Colour: pink to red. Very much like Australian lacewood, a wood that is also sometimes called silky oak. The photograph shows a veneer cut from a silky oak butt. A good choice for exterior work, furniture-making and general interior work. Reasonably priced if you live in Australia, but an expensive option if you live in America or Europe.

BUBINGA
Guibourtia demeusei African rosewood, Cameroon rosewood

A heavy, coarse-textured, straight- to wavy-grained hardwood. Colour: red to purple; red to brown. Comes in good-sized board widths. A good choice for furniture, small carved and turned wares, and for veneers – especially good when you are looking for a rich, dark colour combined with a dynamic grain pattern. Be aware that this is an endangered species.

AMERICAN WALNUT
Juglans nigra Black walnut

A coarse-textured, straight-grained hardwood. Colour: purple to dark brown. A good option for steam-bending, furniture-making, interior work, woodturning, carving, and veneers – it can be worked to a high-shine finish. Good-sized boards are available. In the past it was used for shop fittings, knife handles and gunstocks.

POPLAR
Liriodendron tulipifera Tulip poplar, American whitewood

An even-textured, straight-grained hardwood. Colour: creamy white to yellow; yellow to brown. Good for interior woodwork, furniture, woodturning and carving. Easy to work and can be brought to a good, crisp-edged finish. Burrs or burls are used for fancy woodturning and for decorative veneers.

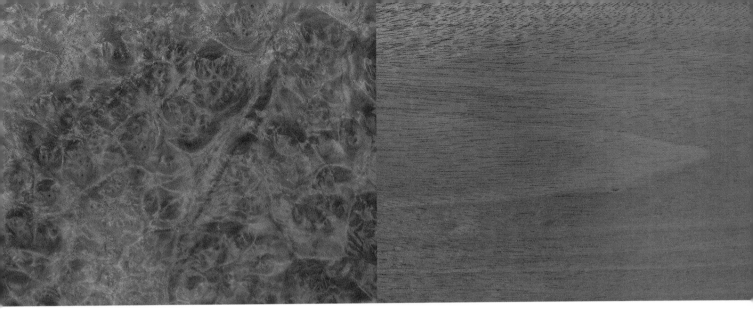

BURR WALNUT
Juglans nigra **American black burr**

A purple to dark brown burr with many of the colour and textural characteristics of the parent tree – a good option when you want to create a decorative veneer detail to go hand in hand with a piece made from solid walnut. Be aware that burr veneers tend to be extremely fragile.

MAHOGANY
Khaya ivorensis **African mahogany**

A straight but loose-grained hardwood. Colour: red to dark brown. Good for both interior and exterior work. As the term "African mahogany" covers all the trees of the *Khaya* species, it is best either to request *Khaya ivorensis* by name, or to settle for what's on offer.

ZEBRANO
Microberlinia brazzavillensis
Zebrawood, Zingana

A coarse-textured, straight- to wavy-grained hardwood. Colour: gold to yellow; brown to black. Though the coarse grain and cavities make it difficult to work, it can, with a lot of effort, be brought to a crisp-edged, high-shine finish. Generally used as an inlay or veneer on small items, and for small carvings and woodturnings.

WENGE
Millettia laurentii **Panga-panga**

A coarse-textured, straight-grained hardwood. Colour: dark brown to black; orange to purple. It is a durable wood, but difficult to work. Wenge is good for flooring, fancy interiors and prestige furniture. Also suitable for carving, turning and decorative veneers.

PITCH PINE
Pinus palustris Florida longleaf, Georgia yellow pine

Coarse-textured softwood; the heaviest of the softwoods. Colour: creamy pink to orange-brown. It is used for large construction projects, joinery, decking and many other outdoor applications.

EUROPEAN REDWOOD
Pinus sylvestris Red deal, Yellow deal, Scots pine

An medium-textured, straight-grained softwood. Colour: pale cream to red-brown. Mostly used for buildings, railway sleepers, telegraph poles, plywood and veneer. The higher grades are used for joinery and furniture-making.

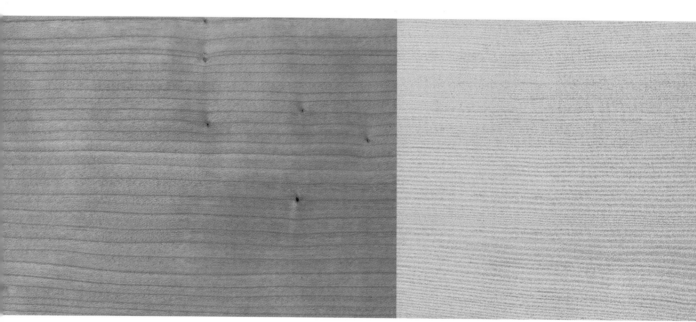

AMERICAN CHERRY
Prunus serotina American black cherry

A straight-grained hardwood. Colour: pink to red; red to brown. American cherry generally has a straighter grain and comes in bigger widths than European cherry. Good for furniture-making, woodturning, carving and steam-bending, and for general hand-tool work. Can be brought to a very smooth, high-shine finish.

DOUGLAS FIR
Pseudotsuga menziesii Columbian pine, Oregon pine

A wavy- to straight-grained, medium-textured softwood. Colour: cream to reddish brown. A top variety for any project where you are looking for a combination of low cost, high strength and long sections. Not easy to work, but can be brought to a hard, crisp-edged finish.

BURR AMBOYNA
Pterocarpus indicus Narra

A hardwood. Colour: red to yellow, to gold to brown. Burr or burl isn't in itself a variety or species of amboyna, but rather a phenomenon that occurs within the tree. The swirling grain makes it a good choice for veneers and woodturning.

AFRICAN PADAUK
Pterocarpus soyauxii Camwood, Barwood

A moderate- to coarse-textured, straight- to wavy-grained hardwood. Colour: purple to brown; golden brown to red. Good for just about anything – furniture, boat-building, woodturning, room interiors, anywhere where you need high strength, a wood that is easy to work, and rich colour.

AMERICAN WHITE OAK
Quercus alba White or pale oak

A coarse-textured, usually straight-grained hardwood. Colour: cream to pink; dark cream to yellow-brown. Much the same as many of the other oaks, apart from the broader variation in colours. A good choice for furniture, room interiors, carving and woodturning.

EUROPEAN OAK
Quercus robur English oak

Coarse-textured, usually straight-grained hardwood. Colour: brown. An extremely popular timber, well known for its character, strength and durability (especially in buildings and boat-building). Excellent for furniture and finishes well. Corrodes in contact with metals: steel fixings and tools, combined with moisture, result in black staining.

BROWN OAK
Quercus robur English oak

Coarse-textured, usually straight-grained hardwood. Colour: brown to dark brown. Has the same properties as European oak but is darker; occasionally the timber in the trunk of the tree is coloured by a naturally occuring fungus which does not affect the strength of the timber. "Tiger oak" is timber with streaks of brown oak running through it.

BURR ENGLISH OAK
Quercus robur European oak

There are more than a hundred different species of oak. Coarse-grained, much like the parent hardwood, burr oak is good for woodturning and decorative veneers. Colour: light tan to red-brown to red. As with other burrs or burls, thin sections tend to be extremely brittle.

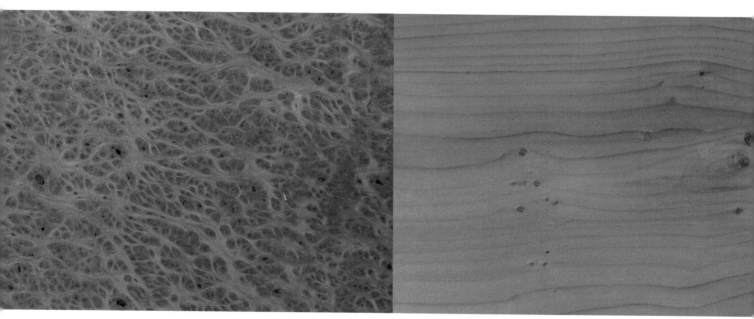

VAVONNA BURR
Sequoia sempervirens
Vavonna burl, Sequoia burr

Vavonna burr is the common name for the burr that grows on the sequoia. It has similar characteristics to the sequoia softwood tree. The texture ranges from hard to soft. Colour: white to red, red to brown. Though sequoia wood proper is almost unusable in section timber form, veneers cut from the burrs – always described as "vavonna" – are highly valued.

ENGLISH YEW
Taxus baccata European yew

A dense-textured, straight- to wavy-grained softwood. Colour: orange to brown; purple to mauve-brown. A durable wood, which is pleasant to work. Very good for steam-bending, woodturning, carving, bow-making, chair-making, and general furniture. The burrs or burls are very good for decorative veneers and fancy woodturning.

TEAK
Tectona grandis
Burma teak, Central American teak

A coarse-textured, straight- to wavy-grained hardwood. Colour: yellow to brown; gold to reddish brown. Difficult to work, but can, with a lot of effort, be brought to a fine, crisp-edged finish. Good for exterior woodwork – doors, shipbuilding, garden furniture and suchlike.

AMERICAN BASSWOOD
Tilia spp. English lime

A smooth-textured, fine-grained, odourless hardwood. Colour: cream to pale yellow. This is the top option for carving and small woodturnings. The grain is so uniform and close that it can more or less be carved in any direction. Traditionally used for small items such as boxes, kitchen utensils, toys – anything that needs a lot of fine detail.

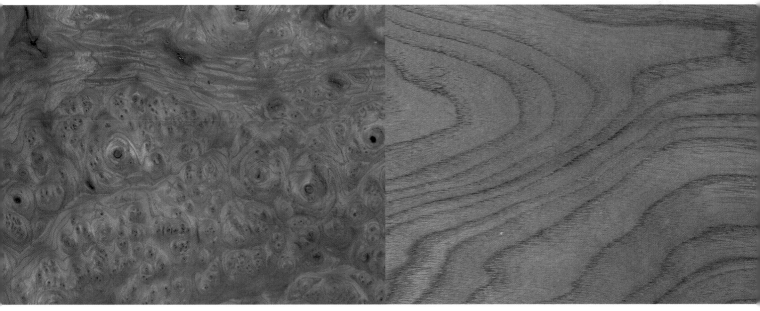

BURR ELM
Ulmus procera Dutch elm, Coffin elm

A coarse-textured, straight-grained hardwood. Colour: red to brown; cream to brown. The photograph shows burr elm, which is a phenomenon that occurs within the tree. Burr wood (or burls) is always more difficult to work than the parent wood. The swirling grain makes it a good choice for veneers and woodturning.

ENGLISH ELM
Ulmus procera Dutch elm, Coffin elm

A coarse-textured, straight-grained hardwood. Colour: red to brown; cream to brown. Elm is excellent for making chair seats for Windsor-type chairs. Available in boards of a small to medium width. Though Dutch elm disease has resulted in short supplies, it is still relatively easy to obtain boards from long-established sawmills.

MANUFACTURED BOARDS

Manufactured boards are made from wood and glue. They include plywood and hardboard types in just about every structural and decorative form that you can imagine, such as blockboard, flake chipboard, particleboard, MDF (medium-density fibreboard) and many other types.

CHOOSING THE RIGHT BOARD

Think carefully about colour, texture, strength and cost, and then bring these factors together for best overall effect. So, for example, you might use low-cost plywood for the back of a cupboard, a structural plywood for an item that needs to be strong, a medium-cost MDF for a surface that is going to be veneered, and so on. You also need to consider how the edges of the boards will be treated.

Blockboard

Blockboard is a stiff and strong material made from strips of solid wood faced with plywood. It can be used for shelves and work surfaces.

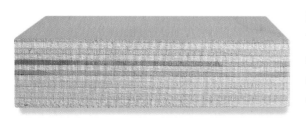

Plywood

Top-quality birch plywood is excellent for furniture-making – it saws well, it planes to a clean edge, and the grain is attractive.

MDF

Medium-density fibreboard – sold in a range of thicknesses – can be used as a substitute for wood in most interior applications.

Chipboard

Chipboard or particleboard is good for interior projects that are variously hidden away, painted or veneered, and do not need to be especially strong.

COMMON SIZES FOR MANUFACTURED BOARD		
Length	Width	Thickness
2440 mm	1220 mm	6 mm
96 in	48 in	¼ in
2440 mm	1220 mm	9 mm
96 in	48 in	$^{11}/_{32}$ in
2440 mm	1220 mm	12 mm
96 in	48 in	$^{15}/_{32}$ in
2440 mm	1220 mm	18 mm
96 in	48 in	$^{23}/_{32}$ in
1220 mm	607 mm	6 mm
48 in	$23^{29}/_{32}$ in	¼ in
1220 mm	607 mm	9 mm
48 in	$23^{29}/_{32}$ in	$^{11}/_{32}$ in
1220 mm	607 mm	12 mm
48 in	$23^{29}/_{32}$ in	$^{15}/_{32}$ in
1220 mm	607 mm	18 mm
48 in	$23^{29}/_{32}$ in	$^{23}/_{32}$ in
1827 mm	607 mm	6 mm
$71^{15}/_{16}$ in	$23^{29}/_{32}$ in	¼ in
1827 mm	607 mm	9 mm
$71^{15}/_{16}$ in	$23^{29}/_{32}$ in	$^{11}/_{32}$ in
1827 mm	607 mm	12 mm
$71^{15}/_{16}$ in	$23^{29}/_{32}$ in	$^{15}/_{32}$ in
2440 mm	607 mm	12 mm
96 in	$23^{29}/_{32}$ in	$^{15}/_{32}$ in
2440 mm	607 mm	18 mm
96 in	$23^{29}/_{32}$ in	$^{23}/_{32}$ in

PREPARED WOOD PRODUCTS

Prepared wood products make life easier. Items such as dowels, mouldings and prepared pine are a good option when you are a beginner. Prepared laminated pine board is more expensive than building the boards yourself; however, you don't have to buy clamps, a machine planer and other equipment.

1 *Laminated pine,* **2** *Hardwood moulding,* **3** *Tongue-and-groove board,* **4** *Hardwood dowel, and various ready-prepared pine sections.*

PREPARED WOOD, DOWELS AND MOULDINGS

Prepared wood has been planed and squared on all faces to a set width. DIY stores usually stock softwood in the standard sizes shown to the right. Some timber suppliers also stock prepared hardwood sections, but these are expensive. Specialist suppliers will prepare wood to any size that you require; they normally supply sections over-long, leaving it to you to cut them to the required length.

Dowels are ready-made round sections of wood, and mouldings are lengths of wood machined into decorative cross-sections. Most DIY stores sell grooved dowels for use in joints, long dowels, and a range of softwood and hardwood mouldings. Many local joinery workshops are prepared to cut complex mouldings to order.

LAMINATED PINE

Laminated pine board (pine sawn into strips and glued to a prepared width and thickness) is perfect for making basic interior furniture and fittings. Many small joinery workshops are happy to make up boards to a specified width, length and thickness. My local joinery is happy to go one step further and to cut, work and build component parts to order. So for example, if I want the end of a cupboard, with a channel on one edge and a rebate on the other, cut and planed to a very precise size and fit, all I do is supply working drawings.

COMMON SIZES FOR PLANED SOFTWOOD		
Width	Thickness	Length
32 mm	12 mm	2100 mm
1¼ in	$^{15}\!/_{32}$ in	82$^{11}\!/_{16}$ in
44 mm	12 mm	2400 mm
1$^{23}\!/_{32}$ in	$^{15}\!/_{32}$ in	94½ in
28 mm	18 mm	1800 mm
1$^{3}\!/_{32}$ in	$^{23}\!/_{32}$ in	70⅞ in
28 mm	18 mm	2400 mm
1$^{3}\!/_{32}$ in	$^{23}\!/_{32}$ in	94½ in
44 mm	18 mm	1800 mm
1$^{23}\!/_{32}$ in	$^{23}\!/_{32}$ in	70⅞ in
44 mm	18 mm	2400 mm
1$^{23}\!/_{32}$ in	$^{23}\!/_{32}$ in	94½ in
69 mm	18 mm	2400 mm
2$^{23}\!/_{32}$ in	$^{23}\!/_{32}$ in	94½ in
94 mm	18 mm	2400 mm
3$^{11}\!/_{16}$ in	$^{23}\!/_{32}$ in	94½ in
119 mm	18 mm	2400 mm
4$^{11}\!/_{16}$ in	$^{23}\!/_{32}$ in	94½ in
144 mm	18 mm	1800 mm
5$^{21}\!/_{32}$ in	$^{23}\!/_{32}$ in	70⅞ in
144 mm	18 mm	2400 mm
5$^{21}\!/_{32}$ in	$^{23}\!/_{32}$ in	94½ in
44 mm	20 mm	2400 mm
1$^{23}\!/_{32}$ in	$^{25}\!/_{32}$ in	94½ in
34 mm	34 mm	1800 mm
1$^{11}\!/_{32}$ in	1$^{11}\!/_{32}$ in	70⅞ in
34 mm	34 mm	2400 mm
1$^{11}\!/_{32}$ in	1$^{11}\!/_{32}$ in	94½ in
44 mm	34 mm	1800 mm
1$^{23}\!/_{32}$ in	1$^{11}\!/_{32}$ in	70⅞ in
44 mm	34 mm	2400 mm
1$^{23}\!/_{32}$ in	1$^{11}\!/_{32}$ in	94½ in
69 mm	34 mm	2400 mm
2$^{23}\!/_{32}$ in	1$^{11}\!/_{32}$ in	94½ in
44 mm	44 mm	1800 mm
1$^{23}\!/_{32}$ in	1$^{23}\!/_{32}$ in	70⅞ in
69 mm	44 mm	1800 mm
2$^{23}\!/_{32}$ in	1$^{23}\!/_{32}$ in	70⅞ in
94 mm	44 mm	2400 mm
3$^{11}\!/_{16}$ in	1$^{23}\!/_{32}$ in	94½ in
69 mm	69 mm	2400 mm
2$^{23}\!/_{32}$ in	2$^{23}\!/_{32}$ in	94½ in

VENEERS AND INLAYS

Veneers are paper-thin sheets of visually dynamic wood that are used to completely cover and decorate a base wood. Inlays are more substantial pieces of exotic wood that are cut into, or placed on, some part of a surface that is usually decorative in its own right.

VENEER PRODUCTS

Veneers are described either by names that point to their source, as with "burr" or "burl", "butt" and "crown", or by names that describe the character or figure, such as "curly", "bird's-eye", "ray", "striped", "coloured" and "reconstructed". Veneers are always unique and less than uniform – a sheet of veneer might be split, have a ragged edge, show insect holes, or have knots. If you buy veneers as seen, the supplier will explain how, depending on your choice, they need to be variously dampened, pressed and edged with gummed tape. Pairs of "matched" veneers are exciting in that they can be used to create all manner of mirror patterns and motifs; the fact that they need to be kept in the order as cut explains why suppliers are sometimes reluctant to give you anything but slices from the top of the stack.

STRAIGHT-GRAINED AND DECORATIVE VENEERS

- **Straight grain** – Veneers cut from the trunk and across the growth rings, resulting in good-sized veneers that are striped along their length.
- **Burl or burrs** – Veneers taken from wart-like growths. The cut results in small dotted and dappled veneers.
- **Butts** – Taken from the base or butt of the tree. The cut results in very fragile, wavy-patterned veneers.
- **Crowns** – These are taken from towards the top of the tree. A characteristic veneer shows a small, dividing, Y-shaped pattern.

A broad selection of straight-grained and decorative veneers suitable for marquetry.

- **Curls** – Curls are taken from the Y-shaped crotch at the top of the tree, resulting in a dynamic, sweeping, U-shaped, feather-like pattern on the veneer.
- **Bird's-eye veneer** – Bird's-eye and other freak figures are taken from damaged or diseased hardwoods, resulting in all sorts of strange but predictable patterns.

COLOURED AND RECONSTRUCTED VENEERS

Dyed veneers have been around for about a hundred years – for example, the grey-stained "harewood" is a bland white wood such as maple, which has been treated. The whole thickness of the veneer is saturated with a colourfast dye. Dyed veneers can be integrated into a design with other dyed veneers, natural veneers and solid wood.

"Reconstructed" veneers are man-made, decorative, real-wood veneers created by an ingenious process that uses dyeing, laminating and slicing to produce colourful patterns. They are expensive, but the results are amazing.

A colourful selection of dyed veneers.

STRINGING, BANDING AND INLAY MOTIFS

These traditional decorative additions are often used on tabletops and cabinet doors. They originally involved the highly skilled and laborious process of cutting and gluing small pieces of veneer; today, however, they can all be bought ready-made.

Stringing (very thin sections of coloured wood inlay) can be used to form a contrasting edge or line, which is good for defining edges or creating panel effects.

Banding (patterned, ribbon-like strips) is often used to enhance the join between different types of wood. Inlay motifs are decorative marquetry designs made from laser-cut, natural-coloured and dyed veneers. Sometimes a 3D effect is achieved by scorching the wood with hot sand. Geometrical designs are referred to as "parquetry". Inlay motifs are expensive but can be made by hand if you have the time.

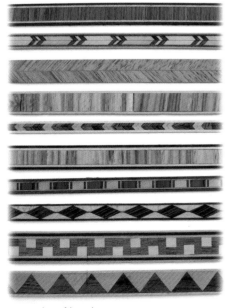

Examples of banding.

These inlay motifs exhibit a range of traditional designs.

WORKSHOP
AND TOOLS 2

SAFETY AND YOUR HEALTH

Woodworking, such as furniture-making, carving, woodturning and toy-making, is an exciting and joyously therapeutic activity, but only if the workshop is clean and well organized, and only, above all, if you are safe. The following pointers will help you create a positive, healthy, user-friendly environment.

A full-face respirator protects your eyes and lungs at the same time.

PROTECT YOURSELF!

High-speed machinery creates a lot of dust, and you need to wear suitable protection – gloves to guard your hands, ear defenders to muffle loud and high-pitched sounds, goggles or a visor to shield your eyes from flying debris, and a mask or respirator to protect your lungs from fine dust and toxic fumes.

Safety glasses

Disposable mask

Ear defenders

Ear defenders and visor

Full-face visor

Mask with face seal and valve

High-spec mask

Respirator and visor

Respirator

Portable vacuum cleaner

Dust extractor

Dust extractor (portable or wall mounted)

Portable dust extractor

Versatile extractor attachment

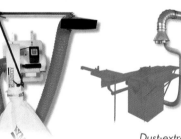
Dust-extraction ducting system

DUST AND CHIP EXTRACTION

Wood dust harms your lungs, clogs machines, and generally creeps about the workshop. Collect it at source with dedicated extractors, and then follow up with a good-quality vacuum cleaner.

A dust-extraction facility for a table saw.

PUSH-STICKS

Plastic push-stick for use with planers, bandsaws and other machines.

A selection of push-pads is especially useful when machine planing.

WORKSPACE

The workspace – the workshop – is where it all happens: every woodworker will have views on the perfect set-up, but there needs to be space to move around, the bench must be sturdy and at the correct height, the lighting, heating and ventilation must be just right, and there needs to be lots of storage.

WORKBENCHES AND TRESTLES

If you make do with a wobbly worksurface that is at the wrong height, your back and your work will suffer. The height of the work surface should be adjusted to about 860 mm (34 in) for a man and 660–760 mm (26–30 in) for a woman. If you enjoy working with hand tools to plane and cut joints, choose the biggest, best-quality and best-equipped bench that you can afford.

Trestles are useful for supporting large boards while you saw them.

LAYOUT, SHELVES AND STORAGE

The more organized and tidy you are, the more space you have to work in. Incorporate shelving, cupboards and racks for tools and wood. If you have limited space, consider combination (multi-purpose) machines; alternatively, use small hobby machines, which are easily moved out of the way after use.

Folding workbench

Light-duty bench

Fold-down bench

High-quality, heavy-duty bench with shelves and cupboard storage

Pair of folding trestles

Overhead storage racks

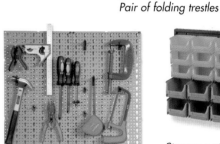
Versatile tool display

Storage system for fixings

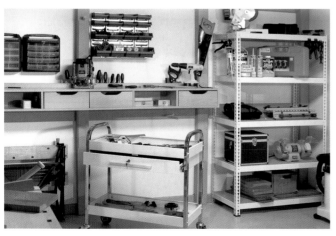
Arrange the storage so that everything is easily accessible.

A small adjustable lamp ideally suited to a workshop environment.

LIGHTING

You need plenty of light in a workshop. The best light to work in is natural light, but in summer the heat and glare might be overwhelming, so consider adding shutters to the windows. Fluorescent tubes are the most efficient type of electric light, but less comfortable for the eyes than ordinary lighting.

Once the background lighting is in place, add adjustable lamps by each work area or machine.

WOODWORKING MACHINES

In the last few years, small woodworking machines have evolved to the point where they really do a very professional job. Design standards have rocketed, there is a huge choice, prices have tumbled – the average hobby woodworker can now easily put together a whole range of top-quality items.

BANDSAW

A bandsaw is a bench-top or floor-mounted machine that has a flexible saw blade in a continuous loop. It is used for cutting curved component parts. In use, the workpiece is set down on the worktable and manoeuvred so that the moving blade is presented with the line of cut. Narrow blades are used to cut tight curves in thin wood; wide blades are better for cutting broad curves in thick wood.

TABLE SAW

A table saw is used for sawing stock to width and length, and for cutting details such as grooves, channels and mitres. In essence, it is a table with a spinning saw disc at the centre, a rip fence to the right-hand side and a sliding or extending table to the left. In use, you true up one edge of the wood, set the rip fence to the desired width, and then use your hands and a push-stick to move the wood through.

Small bench-top bandsaw

A bandsaw blade is a continuous loop, which is supplied and stowed as a collapsed coil; open out with care.

Fine-cutting blade: 10 teeth per inch

Fast-cutting blade: skip pattern, 3 teeth per inch

Light-duty table saw

A high-quality table saw ideally suited to a large home workshop.

Most machines are supplied with a general-purpose saw blade. Veneered boards require a finer blade.

SCROLL SAW

The scroll saw, also known as the fretsaw, is a fine-bladed, bench-top machine designed specifically for cutting small, complex curves in relatively thin wood – up to about 32–50 mm (1½–2 in) thick. In use, the blade is tensioned, then the workpiece is held firmly on the worktable and fed towards the blade.

To cut an enclosed shape (an irregular hole in the centre of a piece of wood), one end of the blade is unhitched and passed through a drilled pilot hole.

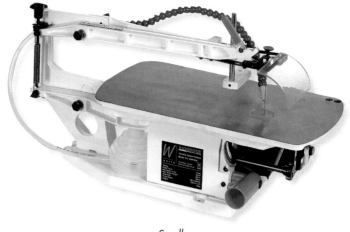

Scroll saw

A sliding compound mitre saw can be pulled forward to cut across planks 305 mm (12 in) wide. The extensions either side support the workpiece.

COMPOUND MITRE SAW

There are all manner of low-cost, top-quality compound mitre saws on the market. In essence, they consist of a disc blade that can be swivelled left to right and/or tilted.

In use – to cut a compound 45° mitre, for example – the mitre gauge is set left or right to the 45° mark, the blade is tilted to the required angle, the workpiece is placed on the saw table, hard up against the fence, so that the line of cut is to the waste side of the drawn line, and then finally the cut is made. Some of the more sophisticated saws are fitted with extras such as depth stops and integral laser guides.

A mitre saw stand, which can be adjusted to take most makes of mitre saw. A good option for a small workshop, and/or if you want to work outside or in a different location.

A compound mitre saw fitted with a laser guide that clearly indicates the position of the cut – a wonderful innovation.

RADIAL-ARM SAW

A radial-arm saw is a cross between a table saw and a compound mitre saw... with extras. In essence, it is a disc saw mounted on a swinging arm or beam, and the whole thing is mounted on a table. In use, the arm is set to the desired angle, the saw blade angle is fixed, and the depth of cut is set; then the workpiece is positioned on the table so that it is held firmly against the stops and guides, and the cut is made. The working action involves the user sliding the whole saw-and-motor unit backwards and forwards along the overhead arm.

COMBINATION SAWS

Radial-arm saw

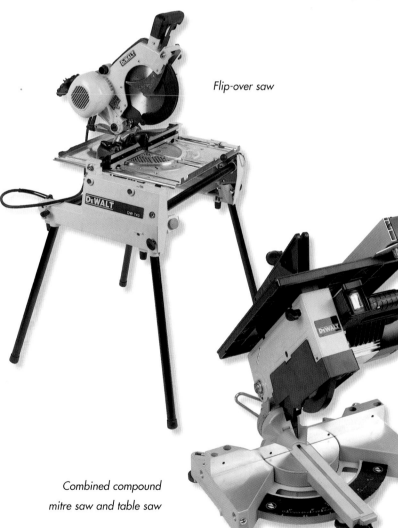

Flip-over saw

Combined compound mitre saw and table saw

PANEL SAW

A panel saw is designed specifically for cutting large sheet materials to size. If you are routinely slicing up sheets of ply, blockboard and suchlike, it is a good machine to go for, but it is unlikely that you will have the space or budget for this machine in a home workshop.

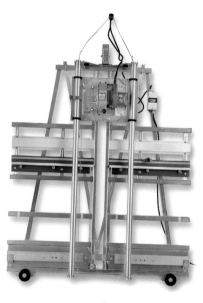

Panel saw

PLANER

A planer, or planer-jointer, is a freestanding or bench-mounted machine that is designed to plane or dress the face side and face edge of a workpiece.

In use, the workpiece is first passed through to achieve one fair side, termed the "face side". Then it is passed through to achieve one good edge or "face edge". Once this operation is complete, it is passed through a planer-thicknesser.

A planer is a good choice if you have enough space for a planer and a planer-thicknesser, but most home woodworkers with limited space opt for a combination planer-thicknesser.

THICKNESSER

Thicknessers come in many shapes and sizes, and may be freestanding, bench-mounted, or portable. The portable machine shown below is great for a small home workshop. In essence, there is a cutting blade and a worktable.

In use, the two table-wings, with their integral rollers, are swung down, the height of the cutter head is adjusted for the first skimming cut, and then the workpiece is fed through. And so you continue, lowering and passing, first one side and then the other, until the thickness is right. As for the machine being portable… yes, it can just about be moved, but it's not very easy!

Planer

Portable thicknesser

Planer-thicknesser in planing mode

Planer-thicknesser in thicknessing mode

PLANER-THICKNESSER

The modern, dual-purpose planer-thicknesser is both beautifully designed and relatively low in cost.

In use, the order of work is to plane the face side, adjust the fence and plane the face edge, and then to put the machine into thicknesser mode and plane the other two surfaces so that edges and sides are parallel and square to each other.

37

PILLAR DRILL

The pillar drill, or drill press, is a bench-top or floor-standing machine that is dedicated to drilling holes. You might think that a good-quality hand-held drill is sufficient for drilling holes, but a good pillar drill will enable you to drill spot-on, perfect holes every time. In use, you fit a drill bit in the chuck, clamp the workpiece to the drill table; set the depth gauge stop, and then pull down on the capstan wheel to bore the hole. A pillar drill teamed with a forstner bit is a winning combination.

MORTISER

A small bench mortiser is, in essence, a small pillar drill with a chisel and auger bit assembly – a bit like a four-square chisel with a drill bit at its centre. In use, the workpiece is clamped in place, and the handle is pulled to cut the mortise. The drill bores the hole and the cutter turns the round hole into a square mortise.

Pillar drill

Radial drill

Mortiser

Mortise chisels

Bench sander

SANDING MACHINES

Sanding machines come in just about every shape and size that you can imagine. There are belt sanders, combination belt and disc sanders, huge sanders that sort out a whole board, oscillating sanders for small finishing tasks, large and small drum sanders, large mangle-like sanders, and so the list goes on.

If you are a beginner, hold back until you know your needs, and then purchase a machine to suit.

In use, you set the various stops and gauges, fit the appropriate grade of abrasive, and pass the workpiece through. Sanders produce huge amounts of very fine and potentially hazardous wood dust, so a dust-sucking machine to take care of the dust is a must. You need to take this additional, but necessary, cost into account when you are making a decision about a machine.

Oscillating spindle sander

Vertical/horizontal belt linisher

Mini oscillating spindle sander

Drum sander

Details of the vertical/horizontal belt linisher: (left) platen in horizontal mode; (right) radius table

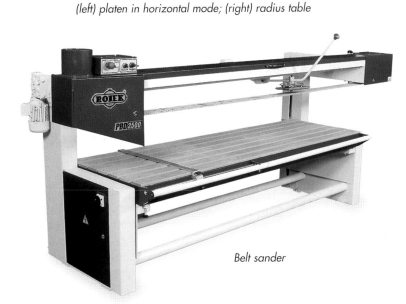

Belt sander

Another make of drum sander

SPINDLE MOULDER

A spindle moulder is used for cutting profiles – such as slots, channels, rebates, complex curves and window sections.

In use, you fit the appropriate cutters, set the fence in place, organize the table, take note of the various warnings, and then run the wood through or past. Spindle moulders used to be thought of as industrial machines really only suitable for professional joinery workshops. Now, however, some of the smaller machines are suitable for home workshops. For example, the machine illustrated allows large-diameter tooling such as panel raising, making mouldings and tenoning, as well as general router-type work. This means it can be used to make things such as picture mouldings, skirtings, kitchen doors, window sections and many other items.

WARNING Of all woodworking machines, the spindle moulder is considered to be the most dangerous. If you are a beginner and thinking about getting such a machine, it is vital to contact a professional woodworker and ask for advice and guidance.

Spindle moulder

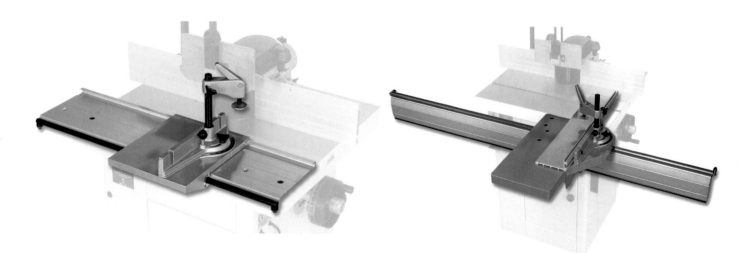

Shown with tenoning table fitted

Shown with sliding table fitted

COMBINATION MACHINES

Combination machine

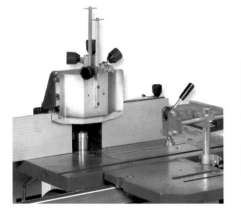

In spindle moulder mode

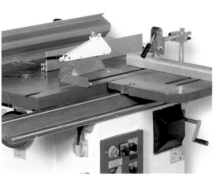

In table saw mode

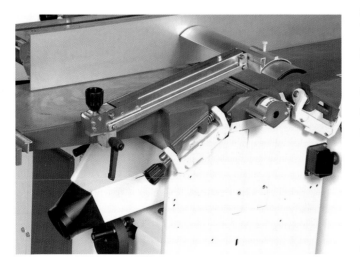

In planing mode

A combination or universal machine brings several machines into a single, carefully designed, compact, multi-functional unit. There are lots of different machines on the market, all with slightly different functions. The machine illustrated can be used for crosscut sawing and ripsawing, planing and squaring, thicknessing, spindle moulding and tenoning. Some machines also include woodturning and fretsawing functions.

If you are a beginner, look at a range of machines, assessing the cost, the number and type of functions, the size of the various motors, and so on. Then look at the single-function machines: planer, thicknesser, lathe, and so on.

If you have adequate space, a range of individual machines might be the best option for you. Or a combination machine might cover your woodworking interests perfectly – perhaps you like making toys, and small woodturning projects. Consider also the extra time it takes to convert a combination machine from one function to another compared to a dedicated machine.

POWER TOOLS

Power tools are amazingly efficient, but only if you are using the right tool for a task. A struggle with the wrong tool may lead you to conclude that woodworking is not for you. Start with a few top-quality essentials: a cordless drill, a jigsaw and a sander, and then get other items when the need arises.

CIRCULAR SAW

A high-quality circular saw – mains powered or cordless – is a very useful tool, well able to cope with the full range of sawing tasks if you fit the appropriate blade. In use, the workpiece is clamped securely in place, the saw is held in both hands, and the cut is made.

WARNING Of course all woodworking tools are potentially dangerous – but circular saws are particularly so. The best advice is to get a top-quality tool that is fitted with a full range of guards, follow the health and safety guidelines, and to work with care.

JIGSAW

A jigsaw (mains or cordless) looks a bit like a hand sander with a flat table on the underside, from which a saw blade protrudes. It is a great tool for cutting straight lines and broad curves in wood up to about 50 mm (2 in) thick.

In use, the tool is held in one hand and its flat underside is positioned on the workpiece, with the blade to the waste side of the line of cut, but not quite touching the wood. The power is switched on and the tool is advanced along the line of cut. The blade jiggles up and down and swings from back to front so that it is clear of the wood on the down-stroke.

WARNING Obviously, keep your fingers away from the blade. Always hold the tool firmly on the workpiece, and always wait for the blade to stop moving before removing the saw from the line of cut.

Circular saw

Jigsaw

Jigsaw blade with a bayonet fitting

PORTABLE PLANER

A portable planer (mains or cordless) is a good tool for removing large amounts of wood in the shortest possible time. It cannot be compared to, or compete with, a beautiful set of hand planes, but it is great for all those DIY tasks where the fast removal of large sections is more important than finish, such as cutting the sides of a garden gate to fit, or for doing work on a boat.

In use, the workpiece is held securely, the depth of cut is adjusted to suit the task, and then the tool is held in both hands and worked with a forward, skimming action in much the same way as with a hand plane. It is important to ensure that the workpiece is free from nails and screws.

It is probably best to start by using a hand plane, and then to get a portable planer if and when the need arises.

DRILL

Always buy the best tool that you can afford, and always go for the biggest chuck size – 10 mm (⅜ in) is good, but 13 mm (½ in) is better. Fit good-quality bits that are appropriate for the task in hand.

You need twist drill bits for all the little everyday holes, spade bits for large, rough holes, and forstner bits for clean-sided, clean-bottomed holes. For drilling and screwing tasks you require a range of countersink, drill and countersink, drill and counterbore, and plug-cutting bits. For fine woodworking, a set of high-quality forstner bits is a must.

Various accessories are available, but much depends on your woodworking needs. A vertical drill stand is good if you are short of space and only involved in general household woodwork, but a good-sized pillar drill is better. A drill-powered woodturning lathe accessory is fine for a small one-off – but only just!

Portable planer

Percussion drill

Drill stand

ROUTER

A router can cut a groove, shape a fancy moulding, cut a rebate, or cut a tongue and groove. It is fitted with a shaped cutter that is the reverse of the profile that you want to cut. The machine can be held in the hand and run forward in much the same way as you might use a hand plane, or it can be upturned and fitted in a router table, in which case the wood is held and manoeuvred so that it comes into contact with the cutter. Most routers have two handles: one fixed and the other in the form of a lock. You set the plunge lock handle to the required depth, hold both handles, and then bear down and push the router forward. In some operations, the base plate is used as a guide, with the side of the plate being run against a straight-edge or jig.

Router – 13 mm (½ in)

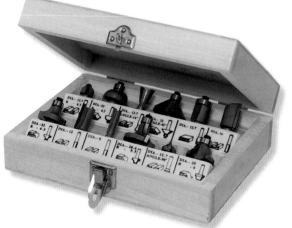

Router cutters

Router table

BISCUIT JOINTER

If you simply want to butt-joint two pieces of wood in the shortest space of time, a biscuit jointer is the tool to go for. In use, you align the component parts that you want to join, set the jointer in place on the workpiece, cut matching slots in the two parts that are to be joined, and then put the biscuits in the glued slots and clamp up. The depth of cut relates to the size of the biscuit.

Biscuit jointer

Biscuits

44

CORDLESS DRILL-DRIVER

Cordless drill-drivers are used both for drilling holes and for driving in screws. The size of the chuck decides the maximum drill bit size. Most drills have a fast-action chuck that allows you to fit and remove a drill bit without a chuck key; also a reverse-action capability that allows you to change the direction of spin – really useful if you are removing lots of screws. The battery takes about one hour to recharge.

Cordless drill-driver

Angled driver

Left to right: crosspoint screwdriver bit, slot-headed screwdriver bit, bit holder

Long screwdriver bit

SANDERS

There are large belt sanders, and small sanders that just about fit in the palm of one hand, and all manner of variations in between.

The sanding sheets are sold according to grit size, sheet size, and sheet shape. A typical range of grades runs from very coarse through to coarse, medium, fine, very fine and superfine.

The cheapest option is a large orbital sander that is designed to take half of a sheet of standard-size sandpaper. Most home woodworkers deal with the dust by fitting the dust bag, wearing a mask, and using a vacuum cleaner to clear up the mess at the end of the day.

Half-sheet sander

Quarter-sheet sander

Belt sander

Finishing sander

HAND TOOLS

There is no denying that power tools take much of the hard work out of the preparation and cutting procedures in woodwork, but against that, hand tools enable you to enjoy a more intimate contact with the wood, and to work in a way that is quieter, more meditative and more individual.

MEASURING AND MARKING

From the outset of a project you will need to use measuring and marking techniques for preparing the materials, establishing dimensions, laying out cutting lines, and testing that faces and edges are true.

Metal tape measure

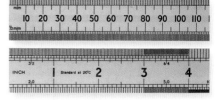

Rule

Try square

Sliding bevel gauge

Mitre square

Dovetail square

Marking gauge

- **Measuring rule** – For reading and transferring measurements. Most woodworkers favour a traditional wooden fold-up rule that has both metric and imperial gradations.
- **Metal tape measure** – A coiled ribbon of sprung steel, which is used for measuring long lengths and curved profiles.
- **Square** – A simple try square, or a carpenter's square, which has two arms fixed at 90°.
- **Bevel** – A tool with two arms that can be adjusted to chosen angles.
- **Scribe and awl** – Pointed tools used to scratch lines and spike holes.

- **Gauge** – Consists of a fence that slides along a beam. The beam has a scribing pin at one end, and the fence has a screw or wedge to hold it in place on the beam. A mortise gauge has two pins – one fixed and the other sliding.
- **Callipers and dividers** – Used for reading and transferring measurements, and for scribing circles.
- **Trammel** – For scribing large circles and large arcs.

Wheel marking gauge

Awl

Trammel

Profile gauge

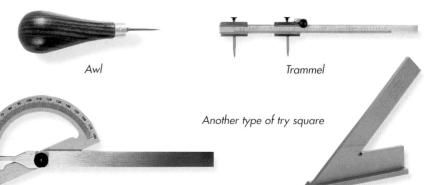

Protractor

Another type of try square

SAWS

Before wood can be planed, laid out with a design, jointed, fretted or shaped, it needs to be sawn to length and width. Start with two saws, a crosscut and a tenon, and only get other saws when the need arises.

Within a specific range or family of saws, such as backsaws, there are many options, each with a particular handle, size and type of teeth. Most wood-workers need only a small number of handsaws, but this will depend on your woodworking interests. The list below will help you evaluate your needs.

A bench hook helps you hold work whilst you saw and is essential if you intend to cut joints by hand.

Ripsaw For cutting along the length of the grain. This is a good choice if you want to convert your own timber.

Crosscut saw For cutting wood across the run of the grain. Most woodworkers have one or more crosscut saws.

Backsaw The term "backsaw" describes a whole family of small-toothed crosscut saws with a strip of brass or steel along the top of the blade. This group includes tenon saws, dovetail saws and beading saws. Most woodworkers start with a medium-sized tenon saw and a dovetail saw.

Coping saw and fretsaw A coping saw is used for cutting small joints and curves in medium-thickness wood; a fretsaw is used for cutting and piercing thin wood. A coping saw is a really useful tool, good for furniture-making, DIY around the house – any situation where you want to cut a curve or a coped joint.

Mitre saw For cutting mitred angles for picture frames, door surrounds and suchlike; however frame mitre saws are fast being supplanted by power saws, which are more efficient.

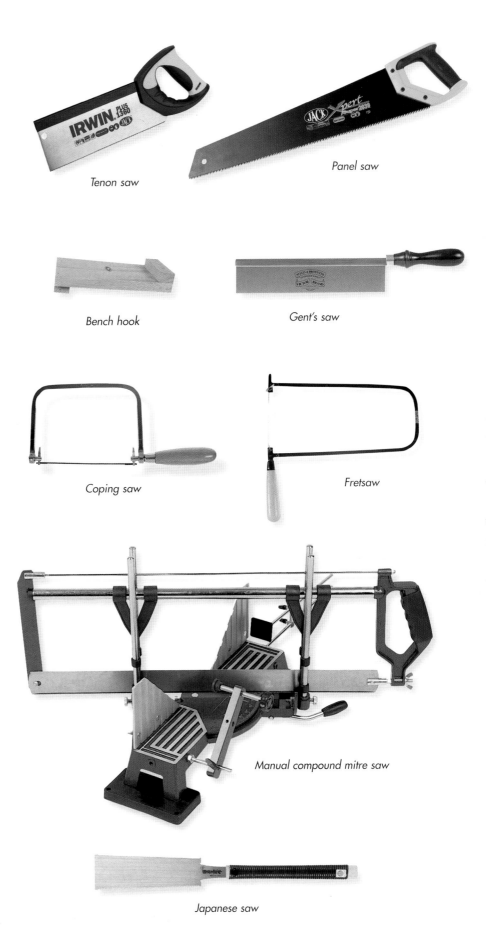

Tenon saw

Panel saw

Bench hook

Gent's saw

Coping saw

Fretsaw

Manual compound mitre saw

Japanese saw

PLANES

Planes are used to cut wood to a smooth finish. Many woodworkers enjoy collecting specialist hand planes and using them to master a range of traditional hand-planing techniques.

At the very least you need two planes: a good smoothing plane for levelling board widths, planing edges, and for skimming and cleaning up the ripples that occur on machine-planed wood, and a block plane for cleaning up end grain and for bringing hand-cut joints to a good finish.

There is nothing so sweat-inducing and tedious as trying to browbeat a dull-edged plane into action. Make sure that you get a top-quality professional tool and keep the blade sharp.

If you wish to plane end grain, you can use a shooting board. This is a home-made jig that helps to hold the work and provides a long straight edge at 90° to the end of the work, along which a bench plane (larger than a smoothing plane) is guided.

A multiplane is a versatile tool with many interchangeable plane blades that produce profiles similar to router cutters.

Rebate planes are used for cutting rebates and perform the same task as a modern router. A bullnose plane is used to trim stopped rebates.

Block plane

Smoothing plane

CHISELS

Chisels and gouges are used for cutting, detailing, and generally paring wood to a smooth finish. A good set of chisels and a range of gouges are essential, but the choice will relate to your woodworking pleasures. For example, a furniture-maker needs a wide range of bevel-edged chisels and mortise chisels for cutting joints, and one or two gouges for scooping out basic curves and hollows; a woodcarver needs a full range of gouges, and a limited number of bevel-edged chisels.

Chisels and gouges are either held in both hands and worked with a paring action, or held and manoeuvred in one hand and struck with a mallet.

SPOKESHAVES AND DRAWKNIVES

A spokeshave is essentially a short-soled plane with a winged handle at each side. A drawknife is an open-bladed knife with a handle at each end. In use, a spokeshave is held in both hands and pushed, while a drawknife is held in both hands and pulled. Both tools work with a skimming, shearing action.

Bevel-edged chisels

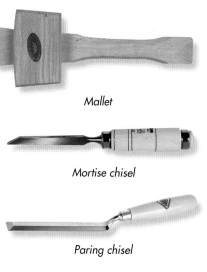

Mallet

Mortise chisel

Paring chisel

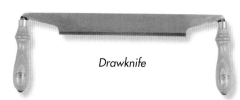

Drawknife

HAMMERS

Most woodworkers use three hammers: a claw hammer for general DIY work, driving in and pulling out nails, and two Warrington-type cross-peen hammers for tapping in small nails and pins. Good-quality hammers are graded according to weight and run from 100–450 g (3½–16 oz). Purchase from a specialist tool supplier.

DRILLS

The traditional brace and twist bit has, to some extent, been overtaken by the power drill, but most fine woodworkers would argue that hand drills allow you to achieve maximum accuracy with the minimum of fuss, noise, dust and effort.

SCREWDRIVERS

Not long ago, woodworkers could manage with a couple of tapering-tipped cabinet screwdrivers and a Phillips crosshead screwdriver. But now screw technology has advanced and a whole range of screwdrivers is required.

OTHER USEFUL TOOLS

There are all sorts of other tools – craft knife, nail punch, pincers, rubber mallet and so on – that are good in their own right. But to start with, buy only essential tools, and get others as you need them.

SCRAPERS

Sprung-steel cabinet scrapers are used for working the surface of wood to an absolutely perfect finish. They are much favoured by cabinetmakers who want to achieve a super-smooth, better-than-sandpaper finish.

SANDING BLOCKS

A sanding block allows you to hold and control abrasive paper while it is in close contact with the wood being worked. Buy ready-made foam, cork or rubber blocks, or make your own and wrap sandpaper around it. Blocks make the tedious job of sanding that much easier.

Pin hammer

Brace

Claw hammer

Offset screwdriver – for awkward places

Screwdrivers

Multi-purpose knife

Centre-punch

Pincers

Rubber mallet

A selection of cabinet scrapers

Scraper burnisher

Cork and rubber sanding blocks

49

CLAMPS

A clamp is a device for holding the wood you are working on securely. Clamps go by many names, such as clamps, hold-fasts, hold-downs, or vice-clamps. As for the number of clamps you need, experience tells me that you can never have enough.

G-CLAMP

Wait until you are faced with a specific clamping task, and then get the type, size and weight of clamp that best suits your needs. Always purchase top-quality items, and always get them in pairs.

CORNER CLAMP

A clamp designed specifically for clamping up lightweight frames and structures – very good when you want to butt-joint two component parts to create a 90° corner.

EDGE CLAMP

Edge clamps are good for clamping batten edgings to boards and sheet material; they can also be used as G-clamps, and for all sorts of other tricky clamping tasks.

G-clamp

Quick-action clamp; clamp/spreader

Corner clamp

Edge clamp

BAND CLAMP

Band or web clamps, used with plastic clamping corners, are a good, low-cost option for clamping up relatively lightweight structures such as picture frames and small boxes.

MORE OPTIONS

There are hundreds of different clamps on the market – some good, some very good, and some really terrible. Think carefully before committing to a non-traditional option such as a clamp that claims to answer all your clamping requirements.

SASH CLAMP

Beam, bar, and sash clamps are used for assembling large frames and structures. Although it is always wise to buy best quality, you can cut costs by getting clamp head sets.

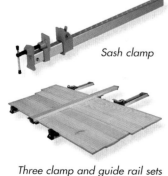

Sash clamp

Band clamp

Four-way panel-clamping system

Three clamp and guide rail sets

Clamp head set

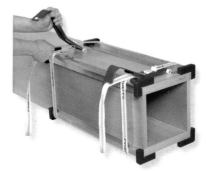

Band clamp clamping system

Toggle clamp

OTHER EQUIPMENT

Woodworkers are forever on the lookout for equipment that will help them to work faster, more easily, at a lower cost, or more precisely. One moment they are happy with a set of gouges, for example, then they need a certain shape of honing stone, another knife, and so on – the search is continually exciting.

CUTTING GUIDES

Cutting guides (clamp and guide rail) provide a firm and straight edge to guide tools such as a jigsaw, router or circular saw. Some guides are designed for all manner of tasks, while others are designed for specific procedures.

Cutting guide used with a jigsaw

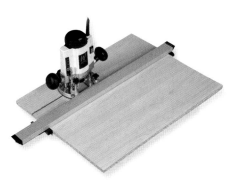
Cutting guide used with a router

ROLLER SUPPORTS

Roller supports or stands are great when you are handling long lengths of wood or large boards that generally need to be eased, guided and supported. Make sure that you get ones that have a failsafe height-adjustment mechanism.

MOISTURE METER

A simple, battery-powered tool for establishing the moisture content of wood – really useful when visiting a timberyard. Most meters have a measuring range of 5–50 per cent moisture content. Press the electrodes into the wood at several locations to get an average reading. Air-dried timber, after seasoning, should have a moisture content of about 15 per cent; kiln-dried timber about 10 per cent.

Roller supports

Roller stand

Moisture meter

MORE USEFUL EQUIPMENT

Masking tape, a staple gun, drill guides, dowel cutters... the more you become involved in a particular area of woodwork, the more additional items you will need, but you won't know quite what until the very last moment. The best you can do is plan out your working procedures and be ready to get other tools and small pieces later.

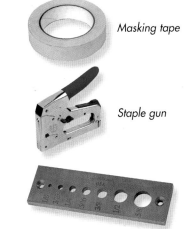
Masking tape

Staple gun

Dowel cutter

TECHNIQUES 3

DESIGN

What is a good design? The answer is wonderfully simple: your design will be good if it is a balanced coming-together of functional needs and creative ideas. The gallery on the opposite page illustrates a broad range of objects and styles where this has been successfully achieved.

INSPIRATION

Artists draw inspiration from their interests and passions, such as romantic love, or the glories of nature; wood designers too must look to their experiences and enthusiasms, whether their interest is in furniture-making, boat-building, toy-making, woodcarving or woodturning.

Let's say, for example, that you want to make a very special one-off chair. Prepare by visiting exhibitions and galleries, looking at the work of other woodworkers, taking photographs, studying books, and generally developing an obsessive interest in the subject of chairs. Then sit down and start thinking about specifics: the size, the type of wood, colour and grain, texture, fixings, making procedures and costs. Your earlier investigations will help you to achieve the best possible design.

DRAWING

Before you start building, sketch out your ideas, options and variations. This will help you to arrive at a design that fulfils a function and provides a challenging woodworking project.

To make sure that a project runs smoothly, you must make scaled working drawings that map out the precise construction of a piece. Start by making sketch drawings on scrap paper, and continue until you have a fair drawing.

Using graph layout paper, look at the size of your item and decide on the scale. If the paper is 100 squares long, you could make each square on the paper equal to one inch. Put the graph

The quickest way to visualize a design is to sketch it; as you think of improvements and new ideas, keep sketching and making notes.

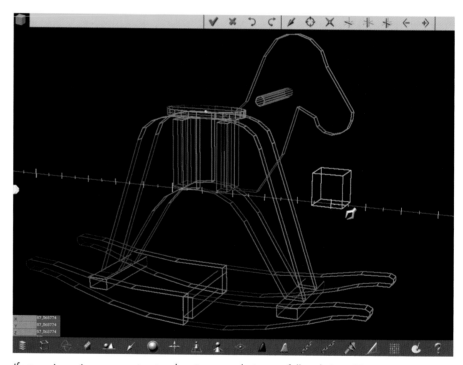

If you enjoy using a computer, try drawing your designs at full scale in a 3D program.

paper over the fair drawing and make modifications. Repeat this procedure until you have a drawing that suits your needs.

Set the drawing under another sheet of graph paper and trace it off with a pencil to make a master plan. Finally, draw out a plan view, a front view, a side view and cross-sections showing details. This process can also be done on a computer.

GALLERY

Featured on this page are some well-conceived and skilfully crafted designs that may inspire your next project!

An elegant turned vessel by Kevin Neelley.

Rose Girl; marquetry by Paul Dean.

Linenfold sideboard *by David Savage.*

Dream-like Love Chairs *created by David Savage.*

Classic furniture design by Bob Dillon.

Sculpture carved from Irish bog wood by Ronnie Graham.

PREPARING WOOD

After making drawings, possibly putting together full-size mock-ups from rough wood or sheet wood, bringing all tools and machines to good order, tidying up the workshop, and deciding on wood type, you are ready for the exciting business of preparing the wood.

PLANKS OF WOOD

For solid wood, you may choose prepared boards and sections, or rough-sawn boards. Either way, you will almost certainly have to saw the wood to length and width, and (to a greater or lesser degree) plane all four sides.

When you go to a wood supplier, the whole place will be piled high with stacks of rough-sawn boards. Each board will present desirable characteristics; also potential problems such as being badly twisted and skewed along its length, or having a diseased sappy edge, twisted grain, wormholes, or too many knots.

Once you have a board without any obvious problems, see if your requirements can be cut from the choice areas. For example, if you need a finished board that is 25 mm (1 in) thick and 305 mm (12 in) wide, check whether the piece of wood is wide and thick enough to allow it to be planed on all four sides.

Of course, much depends on the project – a fine piece of furniture made in English oak is one thing, and a basic pine shelf is another – but always choose wood with care and be prepared to reject wood that shows serious flaws.

SAWING PLANKS BEFORE PLANING

Traditionally, this procedure involved using a large hand ripsaw to slice the wood down the length of the grain – the object being to cut a line more or less parallel to the grain. Most woodworkers now use a circular saw or a table saw.

A waney-edged ash plank and planed samples of oak, maple and beech.

If the wood has a waney edge, draw a line and use a bandsaw, handsaw, or circular saw to cut along it. Once you have one good sawn edge, adjust the table saw's rip fence so that it is parallel to the blade, with the distance between the fence and the blade equalling the width of the board. Don't forget to allow for the width of the saw blade and for planing waste. If the board is generously wide, push the wood through with your hands set well to the back left-hand side of the blade, or use push-sticks.

PLANING

The procedure of surfacing or surface-planing a board means the planing of the face side and the face edge so that they are smooth and at right angles to each other. Traditionally, this was achieved with hand tools – a smoothing plane and a jointer – but it is now more common to use a power planer or a planer-thicknesser.

Hold the board flat down and pass it repeatedly across the cutters until the face side is smooth and flat. Swing the guard out of the way and hold the prepared face hard against the fence. Pass the wood through.

THICKNESSING

After surface-planing a plank (so it has a face side and face edge), the next stage is thicknessing: planing the other side and edge so that all four faces are smooth and square to each other.

This usually involves laying the wood planed-side down on the flat bed of the machine and pushing it into the machine until it is grabbed and fed through automatically. Depending on the power of the thicknesser, 0.5–4 mm (1⁄32–3⁄16 in) of material can be removed in one pass. Continue planing and resetting the machine to produce thinner sections.

Set the machine to remove about 0.5 mm (1⁄32 in) of wood on each pass for a hardwood and 1.5 mm (1⁄16 in) for a softwood (actual setting depends on the power of the machine). Softwood is easier to plane and more material can be removed.

Machine-planing timber successfully requires practice. Follow the manufacturer's instructions and avoid straining the machine.

MEASURING AND MARKING

When the wood has been prepared, a range of tools and techniques are used to transfer the primary measurements, followed by the secondary lines such as angles, circles and flowing forms, to the wood in readiness for making the first cuts.

MEASURING AND MARKING FOR CROSSCUTTING

A crosscut is a cut that runs across the grain at right angles. When using a try square to mark it, put the knife on the measured mark, set the square hard up against the true face edge of the workpiece and slide it up to the knife, and then draw the knife towards you to mark in the line of cut.

When using a compound mitre saw, set the angle scale, adjust the length stop, butt the workpiece hard up against the fence, check that the blade is to the waste side of the line, and make the cut.

It is essential to use the length stop when you are preparing components of an identical length: it is quicker than marking each piece individually and far more accurate.

MEASURING AND MARKING FOR ANGLED CUTS

Make angled cuts with a sliding bevel, which is used in much the same way as a try square. Loosen the wing nut, set the bevel angle against a protractor, tighten up the nut, and then transfer the angle to the workpiece.

Alternatively, use a compound mitre saw. Set the saw blade to the basic mitre angle, then tilt it and set it against the calibrated pivot assembly. Butt the workpiece hard against the fence and stop, and make the cut.

Mark out dimensions and joints using light pencil marks and an accurate measuring rule. Double-check all your markings before starting to cut the wood.

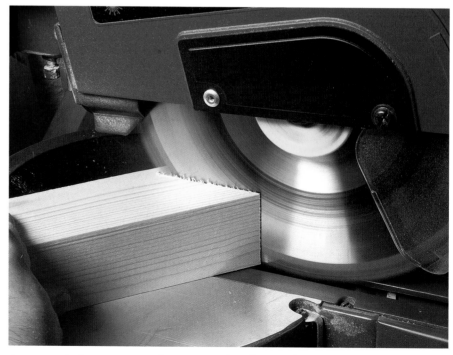

A compound mitre saw is set to the correct angle with an angle scale, saving time.

A compound saw cuts a mitre angle and a tilt angle (a "compound mitre"); both of these can be set using the angle scales on the machine itself.

A grid can be useful for scaling and plotting irregular or "organic" shapes.

CIRCLES AND ARCS

Draw small circles and arcs (part-circles) with a pair of compasses or dividers. Set the two legs to the desired radius; spike one leg on the centre point. Swing the other leg around to scribe the circle.

To draw a larger circle, use a trammel. To make one, use an offcut that is longer than the radius required. Hammer a pin through one end to make a pivot and drill a hole in the other end to take a pencil. (The distance between the pin and pencil point is the radius.)

Set the pencil and spike to the radius of the circle, place the spike on the centre point, and then swing the pencil to scribe the circle. A very large circle or arc can be drawn using a beam compass or trammel head set, which can be clamped to any length of metal tube or wooden dowelling.

ORGANIC SHAPES

Organic shapes can be drawn on wood by eye, or you can use a template.

Sketch the shape on gridded paper, then cut it out to use as a template. If you want to make lots of repeat forms, make a more robust template from sheet material such as plywood or hardboard.

SQUARENESS

To check the squareness of a small internal corner, such as in a drawer or box, the simplest method is to use a try square.

To check the squareness of a large frame, check the corners with a long-armed try square, then use a tape measure to make sure that the two diagonal measurements are equal.

To check the accuracy of a try square, mark a line on a flat surface, then flip the square over and see if you can align the blade with the drawn line. If you cannot, get another square.

SHARPENING

A keen, razor-sharp edge that swiftly shears, slices, skims and chops through wood is one of the great pleasures of woodworking. On the other hand, if you are trying to work with a blunt and chipped cutting edge, it is very hard work and a frustrating experience.

SHARPENING EQUIPMENT

Much depends upon the tool you want to sharpen, but the general sharpening procedure is as follows.

- Grind the blade on a wheel or stone to remove nicks and chips, to square the edge and to establish a new bevel.
- Hone or whet the blade on one or more stones to achieve a new, secondary micro-bevel.
- Polish the blade on a leather strop or grinding-polishing machine.

A sharpening kit should include an electric grinding-polishing wheel, a couple of grinding and honing stones, shaped stones and slipstones for gouges, and maybe a couple of aids to help you maintain good angles.

Wide-wheel bench grinder

Bench grinder

Sharpening kit

Diamond sharpening stone

Chisel-grinding attachment

Honing gauges

Oil slipstone

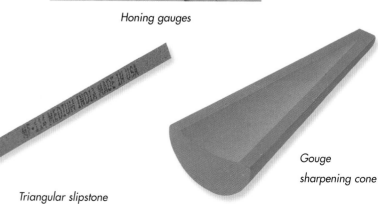

Triangular slipstone

Gouge sharpening cone

HOW TO SHARPEN STRAIGHT CHISELS AND PLANE BLADES

(If the leading edge of the chisel or plane blade is nicked, it has to be ground; otherwise you can miss out this stage and proceed to the stones.)

- Fit the grinder with a fine-grit wheel, adjust the tool rest so that it is horizontal and at 3 o' clock, and set the blade flat on the rest with the bevel uppermost.

- Being careful not to overheat the tool, advance the blade and gently run it from side to side to grind it back to a square edge.

- Adjust the tool rest to the appropriate angle for the blade (say 20°), turn the blade over so that the bevelled face is in contact, and then repeatedly advance the blade and dunk it in a can of water until you have achieved a primary bevel.

- Put the flat face of the blade on a medium water or oil slipstone, dribble water or oil on it, and polish away any roughness. Move to a fine stone, turn the blade over so that the bevel is in full contact, raise the blade a few degrees (either by eye or set it into a honing guide) and then drag it towards you and lift it off. When the blade has been honed and polished, turn it over so that it lies flat down and remove the fine burr.

- Finally, do the same thing on a leather strop or polishing wheel.

- Practise these procedures until you get them right.

HOW TO SHARPEN GOUGES AND CURVED BLADES

Grinding a gouge is much the same as grinding a chisel, the only difference being that the gouge usually needs equal bevels on both sides of the blade. Some woodcarvers also round over the corners of the blade slightly, while others customize just about everything.

Fit the grinder with a fine-grit wheel; adjust the tool rest to an appropriate angle, and set the blade on the rest. Being careful not to overheat the tool, advance the blade so that the bevel is in contact with the wheel, and then roll the handle so that the entire bevel comes into contact.

There are at least four ways of honing the primary outside bevel of a gouge:

- Using an oil or water slipstone, you can run the tool backwards and forwards while rolling the blade.

- You can run the tool backwards and forwards over the stone in a figure-of-eight movement, rolling the blade.

- You can hold the tool at right angles to the stone – with the handle sticking out to the side – and then roll the bevel the entire length of the stone.

- You can hold the tool up to the light and stroke the stone against the bevel while rolling the tool.

- Next, find a slipstone to fit the inside curve of the gouge, dribble it with oil and stroke the inside edge.

- Finally, fold a piece of thick leather to fit the gouge, dribble it with a little oil, dust the oil with fine crocus powder and polish the inside bevel to remove the burr left by honing.

- You may have to modify one or all the procedures to fit the type, curve and character of a particular gouge.

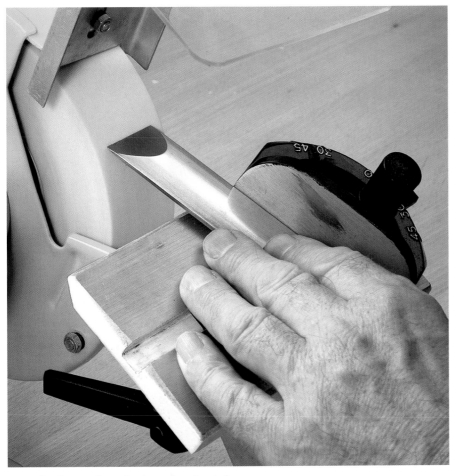

Using the dry grinding wheel on a bench grinder.

CUTTING CURVED SHAPES

Cutting curves in wood is an illuminating procedure. One moment you have a board, and the next you have a curved profile – it may be a curvaceous blank for a table, or perhaps a rough for a duck decoy – and for many woodworkers, the act of cutting a curve is when the creative juices start to flow.

SAWING CURVES

Most woodworkers use a fretsaw, a coping saw or a scroll saw for cutting fine details in thin wood, a jigsaw for cutting rough curves in medium-thick wood and man-made boards, and a bandsaw for cutting broad curves in thick wood.

To use a scroll saw, fit a new blade, adjust the tension until the blade "pings" when plucked, set the workpiece on the worktable, and then advance the workpiece so that the blade is presented with the line of next cut. If you see the blade wandering away from the drawn line, ease back and modify the direction of approach.

To use a jigsaw, set the table part of the saw on the mark; switch on the power and advance to make the cut.

To use a bandsaw, hold the workpiece flat on the table and feed it so that the blade is presented with the line of next cut. It's easy and safe as long as you keep your hands well away from the blade. If you have doubts, use a push-stick to guide the wood through.

A bandsaw is mainly used for cutting curves. Machines are available in various sizes and can accommodate a range of blade widths. Use narrow blades for tight curves.

A jigsaw is ideal for cutting curved and complex shapes.

REPRODUCING CURVES ACCURATELY

Templates are a swift and easy way of reproducing a curve accurately. At its simplest, the template can be a paper cut-out, but when you are working with a router to cut a number of repeats, the template needs to be made from a strong sheet material such as MDF. Make a template that is smaller than the final finished item by the thickness of the router's bush guide.

Clamp the template on to the workpiece, and clamp the whole works to the workbench. Sit the router on the template so that the cutter overhangs and the bush guide is pushed hard up against the edge of the template, and then switch on the power and make the cut. The accuracy of the total cut hinges on the accuracy of the template, the way it is fixed to the workpiece, and the way the router is supported. If, at any time, the greater part of the router overhangs the template, make sure that it is supported on a foot block that is fitted to the underside of the router, or to blocks fitted to the worktable.

ROUTING TECHNIQUES

A good-quality router is a wonderfully versatile woodworking machine, but only if you enjoy working through all the adjustment and set-up procedures required before you start. A router will outpace a hand plane every time, but it must be set up with care and caution.

Edge profile cutters often have a pin or bearing tip that guides the router.

REBATES AND EDGE PROFILES

Fit a plain or self-guided cutter to suit your needs. Clamp the workpiece to the bench. Be aware that you must feed the router against the rotation of the cutter. If in doubt, have a trial run on a piece of scrap wood.

To use a straight cutter to cut a rebate or moulding profile, adjust the side fence so that it is aligned with the underside of the cutter, and make the cut in a series of deeper and deeper passes. Self-guided cutters can be used by simply running the bearing guide against the edge of the workpiece.

GROOVES AND HOUSINGS

Fit a straight cutter. To cut a near-edge through-groove, set the side fence so that the cutter is aligned on the mark. Plunge and lock the cutter, set the base plate on the workpiece, switch on and make the pass. Run right through and switch off. For deep grooves, make a series of deeper and deeper passes.

To cut a housing, clamp a straight-edge guide across the workpiece, and make increasingly deeper cuts. If the housing is wider than the cutter, make the first cut, move the straight-edge to the side and make a second cut alongside the first.

CIRCLES AND ELIPSES

To cut a circle, fit the router to a trammel, use double-sided sticky tape to fix a thin piece of plywood on the centre point, then spike the point of the trammel on the centre of the circle and make the cut.

To cut an ellipse, make a template and cut the ellipse in much the same way as you would cut any other curve.

A router jig for cutting out elliptical tabletops.

JOINTS ON THE ROUTER TABLE

A good way of repeating small, accurate joints is to use a router upside down on a purpose-made router table. The table has a fence guide, cutter guard, spring clamps, mitre fence and various optional extras, and offers a lot of control – far greater than you could achieve with a hand-held router.

Set the router in place on its table, and use it in much the same way as you would use a spindle moulder – set up the various guards and stops and then pass the workpiece through so that the cutter cuts the groove, rebate or halving joint on the underside of the piece being worked.

MORE ROUTING TECHNIQUES

This router jig is used for cutting tenons.

Lettering templates.

LAMINATING AND KERFING

Laminating is the sandwiching together of thin veneers, and bending them around a former to make a curved component designed to be seen from all sides. Kerfing is the bending of a thick section of solid timber to make a curved component designed to be seen only from the convex side.

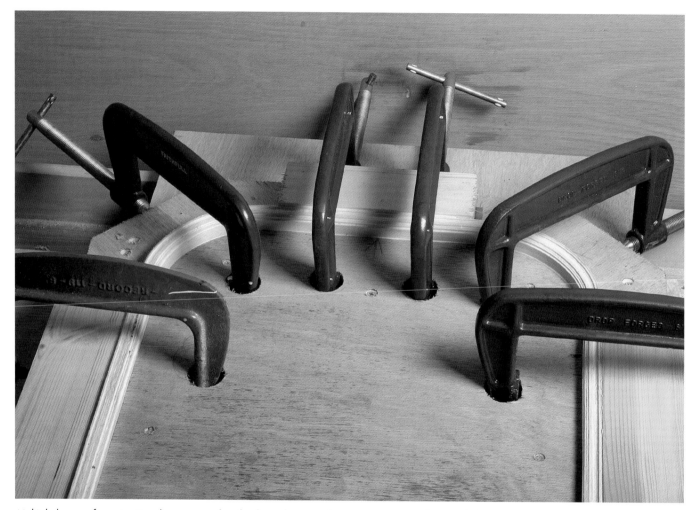

Multiple layers of constructional veneer can be glued together to make strong, permanently curved shapes.

LAMINATION TECHNIQUES
Thin veneers are glued into a sandwich, and then bent around a former and left until the glue has set. This produces a pre-stressed curved component that is designed to be seen from all sides.

The strips can be anything from thin veneers through to just about any thickness that can easily be bent around the chosen curve. There are four designs of former: single, two-part, multi-part and sheet former.

• **Single former** – A simple, convex-curved, bridge-like former. The glued sandwich is bent, bow-like, over the former and clamped in place. Used for simple C-shaped strip laminations.

• **Two-part male-female former** – Two mating shapes that lock together. The glued sandwich is set between the two formers and clamped up. Used to create more complicated, direction-changing, S- and Z-shaped strip laminations.

• **Multi-part former** – Three or more mating shapes that lock around a central core. The glued sandwich is wrapped around the core and the shapes are clamped. Used for complex strip laminations where the ends of the lamination might well come together.

• **Sheet former** – Two wide mating shapes that lock together. The glued sandwich is set between the shapes and clamped. Used to create large, bridge-like forms e.g. chair seats, skateboards.

Designing a single former is pretty straightforward: just make sure that the curve suits your needs. The two-part male and female former, and the multi-part former are more complicated: they cannot be achieved simply by cutting through a solid blank and then separating the two parts – it just doesn't work. You have to determine the thickness of the finished lamination (e.g. 25 mm/1 in thick) and then cut away a parallel strip (25 mm/1 in thick) from the centre of the blank.

As for the choice of wood, you can use veneers, or cut strips from just about any straight-grained, knot- and split-free wood. If you decide to cut your own wood, remember that sawing is both time-consuming and wasteful. Have a few trial runs with various thicknesses, and see what works best for the project.

KERFING TECHNIQUE

Kerfing involves making side-by-side cuts along one face of a thick section of solid timber and then bending the timber towards the cuts. It is best used in situations where the sawn face is hidden from view – such as with a curve-fronted cupboard where the cuts are on the inside, or where the sawn face is covered with veneers, or where two kerfed components are set back to back so that the sawn faces are innermost.

The kerfed component needs to be held in place until the glue has set. You can either use formers and clamps, or you can fix the component directly to a rigid frame or carcass, as with the bottom curved riser on a staircase.

Two factors decide the minimum radius and the smoothness of the curve: the thickness of the saw cuts, and their proximity to each other. The thicker and closer the cuts, the tighter and smoother the curve. It is easiest to use a power saw to make the kerfs (saw cuts). Not only does it allow you to set the fence, depth gauge and end stop, so that all the cuts finish up the same depth, the same width apart, and parallel, but it releases you from trying to make dozens of identical cuts by hand.

There are so many variables that it is vital to have a trial dry run before you start a project. Experiment with kerfs of various widths, depths and spacing, and you will see that the smoothest curves are achieved when the inner edges of the cuts allow the mouth of the kerfs to close and touch. On very fine work, this can be achieved by filing the mouth of the kerfs so that they are V-shaped in cross-section.

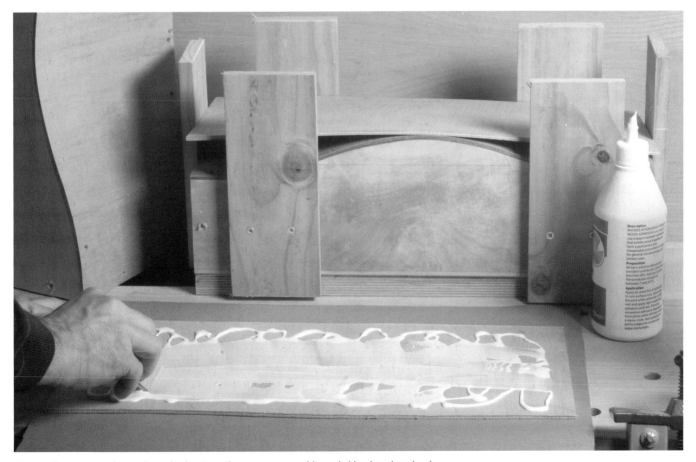

Sheets of veneer or plywood can be laminated to create curved boards like this chair back.

STEAM-BENDING

This ancient woodworking procedure brings about such a transformation that it is almost magical. One moment you have a straight piece of wood, and the next, after subjecting it to lots of steam, you have a beautifully curved piece of wood. It is an exciting, but slightly hit-and-miss woodworking technique.

HOW STEAM-BENDING WORKS

Some woods, because of the unique shape and structure of their cell walls, can be made plastic and pliable by steam. In the pliable state, when the fibres are soft, such woods can be eased into a shape by being bent over a former. Once the wood has cooled, it retains the curved shape. Traditionally, beech and ash were made into chair backs for Windsor chairs and various component parts for Thonet chairs.

The success of steam-bending hinges on five main factors: the type of wood, the length of time the wood has been cut, the thickness of the piece being bent, the steaming time, and the desired curve. The thinner and greener the wood, the longer the steaming time; the broader the curve required, the easier it is to bend the wood. Bending wood for a Windsor chair back is surprisingly easy. Steam-bending is one of those techniques where there is no other way forward than to learn by trial and error.

HOW TO BUILD A STEAM BOX

Depending upon what you want to bend, design the size of the box to suit. A box with internal dimensions of 180 x 15 x 15 cm (6 ft x 6 in x 6 in) is likely to be adequate for most furniture-making applications.

Make it from a double skin of exterior-grade plywood, with a 75-mm (2¹⁵⁄₁₆-in) cavity filled with fibreglass loft insulation. Design it so that there is a steam feed pipe entering from beneath in

Beautiful, traditional Windsor chairs by Bob Dillon. The simple bow and the bow with compound curves are made using the steam-bending technique.

a central position (or at the back end), a safety vent on the top and a door at the front end. For the boiler, construct a special metal box as shown, or use an electric wallpaper stripper. It is recommended that you site the steam box outdoors, NEVER leave it unattended, NEVER allow it to boil dry and keep a fire extinguisher nearby.

HOW TO BEND A SIMPLE BOW

The easiest way to bend a bow is with a metal "bending strap". This is a home-made device (if you are going to do a lot of bending, ask a metalworker to make one for you) consisting of a strip of thin, flexible stainless steel about 30 cm (1 ft) longer than the workpiece. A handle and "stop" are welded or bolted to each end (see photo). The strap constrains the wood during bending to stop it splitting. It is placed on what will become the outside of the curve and causes the wood to compress (pucker) on the inside of the curve. After bending and cooling, the strap can be removed. Make a former (to the shape required) and prepare pegs and peg holes to hold the bow in position on the former once it has been bent.

Sit the workpiece on short lengths of wood to allow the steam to circulate around all sides. Put planed green (unseasoned) wood in the steamer for an hour per inch of thickness. Turn off the steamer. Put on some thick gloves and open the door, keeping your face turned away. Take the workpiece out, locate it in the bending strap and bend it around the former. Work quickly: removing the wood to finishing the bend should take no longer than thirty seconds.

WARNING This procedure is potentially dangerous – work with care and caution, and ask a friend to help.

This steam box uses stainless-steel parts and a gas burner; the liner and boiler were made by a metalworker. An insulated plywood box retains the heat.

A bow shape is bent around a former with the help of a flexible stainless-steel strap; the strap and the sockets at either end restrict the wood, preventing it from splitting.

DRILLING HOLES

The woodworker is forever needing to drill holes – swift holes for nails, countersunk holes for screws, deep holes for dowels, large, smooth-sided holes for design features. Each needs to be worked with care. The perfect hole relies on the choice of drill bit more than anything else.

TYPES OF DRILL BIT

Twist bits for wood and metal. Also available with a pointed tip (for drilling wood) and referred to as spur or brad point bits.

Forstner bits – used to drill smooth-bottomed holes with a perfect finish.

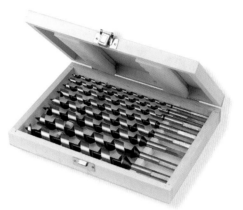

Auger bits – used to drill deep holes.

Combination twist bit and countersink.

CLEAN, ACCURATE HOLES

The forstner drill bit is the perfect bit for boring smooth-sided, clean-bottomed holes. Most bits are guided by their centre point, but the forstner bit is guided by its rim. It can be used at almost any angle and is capable of boring a hole that runs off the edge of a board. Best used in conjunction with a pillar drill, with the workpiece clamped in place.

Flat bits – low-cost bits used to drill large holes.

Plug set – for drilling and plugging holes.

Hole saws – for cutting extra-large holes.

Snail countersink – for drilling perfect countersunk holes.

Tapered hole-cutter – for drilling tapered holes.

Combined drill-countersink – used to drill ready-to-screw holes.

68

NAILS, PINS AND SCREWS

There are hundreds of nails, pins and screws on the market, designed for specific applications. The secret of success is choosing the one that is most appropriate for the task in hand, and then knocking or driving it home with the right tool and in the correct way. See page 82 for more fixings.

A SELECTION OF NAILS, PINS AND SCREWS

1 *Oval wire nail. For carpentry; head can be punched below the surface.*

2 *Round wire nail. For carpentry.*

3 *Panel pin. For fixing mouldings.*

4 *Oval pin. For fixing small pieces.*

5 *Veneer pin. For fixing veneers.*

6 *Cross-headed, countersink, zinc-plated woodscrew.*

7 *Alternative cross-headed, countersink, zinc-plated woodscrew.*

8 *Cross-headed, countersink, stainless-steel woodscrew: outdoor applications.*

9 *Cross-headed, round-headed woodscrew. For fixing hardware.*

10 *Slot-headed, countersink brass woodscrew. For traditional fixing (resists corrosion).*

11 *Slot-headed, round-headed brass woodscrew. For fixing hardware.*

12 *Slot-headed, raised-headed brass woodscrew. For fixing hardware.*

13 *Cross-headed, round-headed black woodscrew. For fixing hardware.*

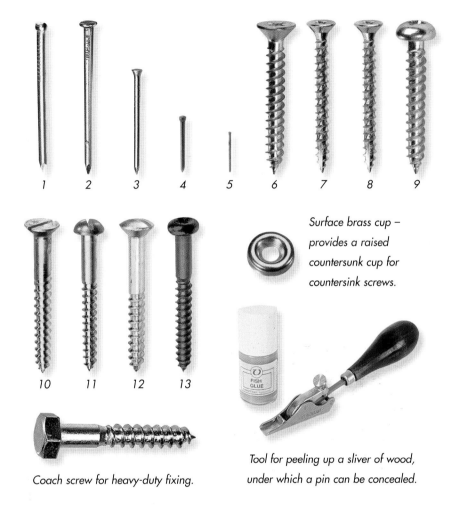

Surface brass cup – provides a raised countersunk cup for countersink screws.

Coach screw for heavy-duty fixing.

Tool for peeling up a sliver of wood, under which a pin can be concealed.

There are round wire nails with flat heads, oval nails, lost-headed nails, panel pins, steel pins, brass pins, nails and pins designed to be used with power guns, and others too numerous to mention. Flat heads are good when you don't mind having the heads on show, lost-headed nails will disappear below the surface of the wood, brass is good when you are worried about corrosion or where you want a decorative effect (but steel nails are stronger than brass).

There are slot-headed and cross-headed steel, brass and plated screws. There are screws with round heads, countersink heads, hex spanner heads; screws with fast threads; stainless-steel screws for use in corrosive situations, and so on.

Always go for a screw that is about twice as long as the thickness of wood to be fixed, but not so long that it breaks through the other component. Whether you opt for nails or screws depends

upon what you are making. Some traditionalists only like slotted screws. Cut steel nails look just right in floorboards; hand-made rose-headed nails look good in folk-art woodwork. As well as being functional, a nail or screw is as much a design feature as wood colour and texture.

For low cost, speed and convenience, use cross-headed, twin-threaded countersink screws; these are ideal when the screwheads can be concealed.

GLUING AND CLAMPING

After preparing all the component parts for a project, it is time for a trial assembly. The idea is that you have a dry run put-together (i.e. without glue), complete with screws and clamps, to make sure that you haven't made any mistakes – which would be difficult to sort out when the pieces are smeared with glue.

GLUE OPTIONS

Today there is a vast range of glues and adhesives.

- **Animal glue** – Good for fine traditional furniture, when there is a need for authenticity.
- **PVA adhesive** – A low-cost, general-purpose option, ideal for most woodworking tasks.
- **Urea-formaldehyde adhesive** – General-purpose water-resistant glue, good for filling small cavities.
- **Resorcinol glue** – A completely waterproof two-part glue, good for rough work.
- **Polyurethane glue** – A waterproof glue that expands slightly as it cures. Very stable.
- **Contact adhesive** – A good choice when you want to achieve an instant bond.
- **Cyanoacrylate glue** – Also known as superglue; good for instant fixes and repairs, much favoured by woodturners, carvers and toy-makers.

PREPARATION

A successful glue job relies on preparation. It is tempting to attempt to get a job done quickly, but try to avoid gluing up in a rush.

Check the joints: the mating surfaces have to be smooth, flat and free from dust. Do a trial dry-run fitting – assemble the components without glue to check that the joints close up and the structure is square. (In some cases, such as dovetail joints, avoid assembling the components fully because if you have to

knock them apart it could damage the joint. Just be sure they will fit by offering the parts together and checking by eye.) Read the glue manufacturer's directions carefully, fill a bowl with water, and have a clean white cotton cloth ready. Set and arrange the clamps and protective pads for the clamp heads.

It is a common mistake to use too much glue. This results in masses of glue squeezing out, which takes ages to clear up and may fill the pores in open-grain wood or end grain – and this will resist the subsequently applied oil or lacquer and leave a patchy finish. Too little glue will result in a weak joint, so try to achieve a balance.

HOW TO GLUE AND CLAMP A TABLE FRAME

After a trial dry-run assembly, disassemble the frame and put the components aside. Take two legs and the rail for one side; spread glue on the mating faces and clamp up. Check with a square and rule, and then adjust the clamps accordingly.

Repeat this procedure with the other two legs and rail. When the glue has set, take the two mirror-imaged assemblies and glue and clamp them together. Make checks with the square at every stage along the way.

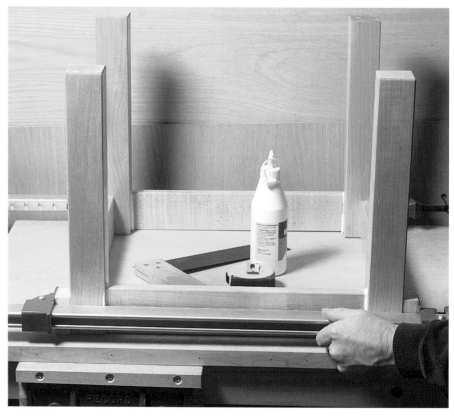

A table frame; the components can be varnished before they are glued together.

HOW TO GLUE DOVETAIL JOINTS

Do a trial dry-run assembly, check that the cuts are free from debris, and then spread glue on the mating faces. Clamp up and check for squareness.

Excess glue will almost certainly ooze from the joint. Wipe it away with a dampened cloth unless it's a high-quality piece; if so, leave the glue to dry and scrape it off when it's cured. The scrape-off approach avoids the wiping of glue into the grain – a really bad idea if you want to apply a delicate finish.

HOW TO GLUE A CHAIR FRAME

The problem with gluing a chair frame (a traditional kitchen chair with a turned leg and slab seat) is that the curved component parts are difficult to clamp. Use either a traditional cord-and-stick-type tourniquet clamp or one of the new ribbon clamps; or make shaped blocks so that you can use sash clamps. One or more dry runs will show you the way.

HOW TO GLUE DOWELS AND BISCUITS

The challenge, when gluing dowels into holes and biscuits into slots, is applying the glue in the shortest possible time, and controlling and directing the glue (dowels and biscuits expand at such a rate that they very quickly become unusable).

Often it is better to glue up in two or more stages (rather than all at once).

Glue applicators (left to right): roller, biscuit joint applicator, dowel joint applicator and brush applicator.

Much depends upon the project, but a good way forward is to start by spreading the glue on the mating faces of the joints, rather than in the holes or slots, and then to use a long-nosed applicator to aim the glue directly into the hole or slot. You can then swiftly wipe a small amount of glue over the biscuits or dowels and then just as swiftly clamp up.

RUNNING REPAIRS

Always think very carefully about the choice of glue for a project. White PVA-type glue is good for most jobs, but sometimes you may need a waterproof or fast-setting glue.

If you were carving a small figure or turning a small item, and suddenly a part split off, you could use PVA glue and wait overnight for it to set. But you would probably prefer to make the mend and continue working, so the best option would be cyanoacrylate glue, otherwise known as superglue.

Gather up the part(s), making sure you have all the bits, brush dust and debris off the mating surfaces, and test for best fit. Work out how you are going to clamp the parts together – you could simply hold them, or strap them up with masking tape – and then swiftly apply the glue to both faces and clamp up. If you get it right, the glue will set in less time than it takes you to wash your hands and have a cup of tea, and you will be able to get on with the job.

Make absolutely sure that you don't get the glue on your skin, especially on your face.

EDGE-TO-EDGE JOINTS

Before there were so many man-made boards on the market, the only way to create a large, stable slab, such as for a tabletop, was to join or joint lots of narrow boards edge to edge. Now, edge-to-edge joints are reserved for pieces of quality furniture where there is a need for a solid wood panel.

PREPARATION

Take the narrow boards (all nicely surfaced and edge-planed) and set them side by side so that you can view them end-on. Look closely at the end grain and rearrange the boards so that the end patterns alternate – dip-rise-dip-rise.

Look at the whole arrangement and turn selected boards on their axis so that from one board to the next the grain is always running in the same direction. Pencil-number the boards so that the order is clear. Take neighbouring boards – say 1 and 2 – and set them back to back so that the numbers are on view. Use a square to check that they are true. Refold them so that the edges are in contact and hold them up to the light. The line of light should be minimal and

thin. Repeat with all neighbouring boards – 1 and 2, 2 and 3, and so on. If one of the joints shows too much light – indicating a peaked edge – pencil-mark the problem area and make adjustments with a hand plane or planer-thicknesser.

BUTT-JOINTING METHOD

Plane the faces and edges square, arrange the end grain so that it dips and rises, and pencil-number the boards so that you can see how they relate and fit to each other. Bridge the boards, edge to edge, over a couple of battens. Set two clamps in place, complete with protection blocks between the clamp heads and the workpiece, and clamp up. Turn the panel over, set the third clamp across the middle, and clamp up.

When all is correct, disassemble the pieces, spread a thin layer of glue on mating edges and reclamp as described.

BISCUIT JOINT METHOD

Plane the faces and edges square, arrange the end grain so that it dips and rises, and number the boards so that you can see how they relate and fit to each other. Square up the arrangement and clamp up. Take a square and run centre-lines across the width of the boards, then remove the clamps. Set the cutting depth of the jointer to suit the thickness of the wood and the size of the biscuits, then systematically set the tool against the various centre-lines and make the cut. Finally, glue the slots and the biscuits and clamp up.

Gluing boards edge to edge is easiest when the boards are perfectly prepared with square edges and faces – otherwise you will get gaps!

EDGING BOARDS

Edging or edge-lipping is a simple technique that involves fronting the edge of a man-made board with a decorative strip of solid wood, or a strip of solid wood that will be covered with a veneer. This makes the board appear to be a more expensive material; it also protects the edge of the board from damage.

EDGE OPTIONS

- **Direct veneer** – Good for edges with smooth cores, such as MDF and top-quality plywood. Bring the edge of the board to a crisp finish, iron on a ribbon of pre-glued veneer that is slightly wider than the board, then rub back to a good finish.

- **Veneered solid wood** – Edge the core with solid wood (glue or pin in place), then glue a veneer to the strip.

- **Butted square edging** – Glue a square section or strip of solid wood directly to the edge of the man-made board. This is a good option for simple scenarios such as shelves and counter tops.

- **Tongue-and-groove edging** – Like butted edging, inasmuch as the square section or strip fronts the board, but different in that the edging is fixed by means of a tongue or with biscuits.

- **Moulded edging** – A choice option when you want to create a decorative effect, as with, say, the front edge of a shelf, or a nosing on the edge of a stair tread.

IRON-ON VENEERED EDGE

Iron-on veneers (rue or faux veneers) are sold in ribbon-like rolls. Square up the edge of the core board, select a veneer that is slightly wider than the board to be edged, set the ribbon of veneer in place, and then iron it on with a standard domestic iron. This is a swift option for smooth cores that are going to be used decoratively in a situation where there is little risk of the edging getting knocked.

A quick, modern way to achieve a presentable edge is to use iron-on veneer. The drawback is that it is easier to damage than a solid edge.

SOLID EDGE

Solid edge strips are good for edging boards that are themselves already faced with a veneer, such as a sheet of birch-faced plywood. Prepare the edge of the board, glue or glue and pin the edging in place so that it stands slightly proud of the surface of the board, and then plane and rub it down to a good finish. You can leave the edging in its square state, or you can work it to a round or chamfered finish.

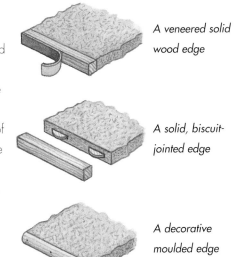

A veneered solid wood edge

A solid, biscuit-jointed edge

A decorative moulded edge

CUTTING JOINTS

The act of cutting and shaping one or more pieces of wood so that they come together is called jointing. The primary objective is to create a functional form, but some joints are so pleasing to the eye that they are used as a decorative feature in their own right.

CHOOSING THE RIGHT JOINT

A joint serves a practical need and it must be strong and fitting for its purpose. However, some joints are so decorative that sometimes they are put on show as a feature.

Let's say that you are going to make a chest. A simple glued and dowelled butt joint is fine if the chest is going to be made of softwood that will be painted, but if it's going to be made of oak and will be on show, a visually exciting joint can be used to good effect.

JOINT PROPORTION AND DESIGN

If we take it that form follows function – meaning the shape of a joint is secondary to its purpose – then for maximum strength you need to achieve a balance between the amount of wood that you cut away and the thickness and width of a member. For example, if you were making a loose-wedged mortise and tenon joint, and you cut more than two-thirds of the wood away from the tenon, so that the tenon is less than one-third the width of the member, the joint would be weak.

Look at the way that the various members are going to come together, and then make sure that no member loses more than about half to two-thirds of its body.

HAND-CUT JOINTS

The act of cutting a joint by hand results in a joint that is less than perfect. This is

Perfect hand-cut dovetails by furniture-maker Alexander Brady.

not to say that it is sloppy, badly fitting or badly cut, but rather that the various facets and forms show slight differences from each other. Beauty is a matter of personal interpretation, but most fine woodworkers say that it is these slight differences that make a hand-cut joint so special.

MACHINE-CUT JOINTS

Machine-cut joints are a swift means to a functional end. If you simply want to get

the job done and you enjoy using machines, machine-cut joints are the answer. The quality of machine-cut joints hinges more on the type of machine and the time and trouble you take over the initial setting up than on anything else. Most joints can be cut on a machine, but it is easier to cut "through" joints such as rebates, housings, bridle joints, through-dovetails, and mortise and tenon joints, than to cut semi-secret joints such as mitred joints and lapped dovetails.

BUTT JOINTS AND REINFORCED BUTT JOINTS

A butt joint is a simple joint where two members join each other, usually at right angles – as with the corner of a chest where the end of one side meets the surface of another side at right angles.

Making a simple square-end butt joint

Step 1: Prepare and square both members so that all edges and faces are square and true to each other.

Step 2: Measure the length of the members and use a square and knife to run shoulder lines all the way around.

Step 3: One piece at a time, support the workpiece hard up against a bench hook and use a fine-toothed saw to cut to the waste side of the shoulder line.

Step 4: Hold the workpiece against a shooting board, and use a finely set block plane to trim the sawn end to a smooth, square finish. Rerun these procedures with all the component parts.

Step 5: Check for a good fit and have a dry-run clamping. Check for squareness.

Step 6: Brush away the debris, spread a small amount of glue on mating faces and then clamp up.

Alternative techniques If you don't have a shooting board, secure the workpiece upright in a vice, with a piece of waste wood to the back and front. Use a small clamp to hold the waste pieces hard up to the sides of the workpiece. Take the finely set block plane and skim the sawn end back to the scribed line. The waste wood prevents the sides of the workpiece splitting off.

A pinned butt joint

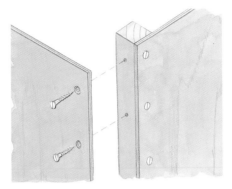

Batten and screws

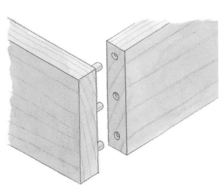

Dowelled joint

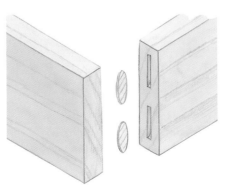

Biscuit joint

Making a simple dowelled frame joint

A frame joint is a joint where two members join each other at right angles to make a T-shaped configuration.

Step 1: Prepare both members so that all edges and faces are square.

Step 2: Measure the length of the members and square shoulder lines all the way around.

Step 3: Secure one member upright in a vice, with pieces of waste wood clamped to the back and front. Use the block plane to skim the sawn end back to the scribed line.

Step 4: Use a measure and square to establish the position of the dowel centres on the end of the members.

Step 5: Bang pins in the centres and clip them off with a pair of pliers – so that you are left with two points.

Step 6: Align the member with the other member and push it home so as to mark matching holes. Remove the pins.

Step 7: Clamp the workpiece(s) in the vice and bore the holes with an appropriate bit.

Step 8: Dribble a small amount of glue in the holes, wipe glue over the dowels and clamp up.

A dowelling kit includes a drilling jig and metal dowel hole centre-markers.

HOUSING JOINTS AND GROOVES
Housing joints

A housing joint is a groove or channel that runs across the direction of the grain and houses the end of a board.

An open housing or through-housing shows on the front edge of the board that is being worked, while a stopped housing joint stops short of the edge – so that the front edge of the workpiece shows as a smooth, unbroken edge.

Making a hand-cut through-housing

Step 1: Measure off the width of the shelf to be housed, and use a measure, square and knife to transfer the measurements to the workpiece. Aim for a tight fit.

Step 2: Decide on the depth of the housing and run the two parallel scribed lines on to the edges of the workpiece. Use a marking gauge to link up the ends of the lines.

Step 3: Being mindful that the housing must stay to the waste side of the scribed lines (between the two parallel lines), take a sharp, bevel-edged chisel and cut V-shaped guide grooves to the waste side of the lines.

Step 4: Use a fine-toothed tenon saw to cut the depth of the housing, then follow up with a chisel and skim the waste down to the depth of the gouged line.

Alternative technique Simply set up a table saw and clear the housing with a series of side-by-side repeat cuts. The same job can be carried out using a sliding compound mitre saw, radial-arm saw, router and router table. It pays to get the setting right by practising on offcuts of the same section that you will be using.

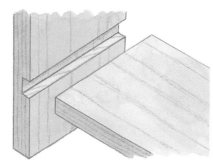

Through-housing

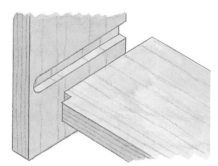

Stopped housing

Tongue-and-groove

Through-groove

Grooves

A groove is a channel – much like a housing – that runs in the direction of the grain, such as a groove along the edge of a tongue-and-groove board, or a groove on the side of a board.

Cutting a groove with a multiplane

Step 1: Take your chosen multiplane (I use a Stanley 45) and fit it with an appropriate cutter.

Step 2: Secure the workpiece in the vice, face edge uppermost.

Step 3: Adjust the plane's fence so that the cutter is centred on the edge; adjust the cutter so it makes a fine, skimming cut. Adjust the depth gauge or foot.

Step 4: Now (this bit is slightly tricky) start at the end of the workpiece furthest away from you, and cut the groove with a series of backing-up cuts.

Step 5: Continue making repeated passes, all the while backing along the wood.

Step 6: When the plane is at the end nearest to you, make a couple of complete passes to clear the groove from one end of the workpiece to the other.

Alternative techniques If you enjoy working with old metal planes, there is a very nice tool – a Stanley 49 – that is designed for cutting tongues and grooves. Its fence can be pivoted one way for cutting tongues and the other way for cutting grooves.

If you prefer to use a quicker method, use a router fitted with a straight cutter of the correct diameter. If the groove is deep or wide you may need to make several passes, resetting the router each time. If the workpiece is short or small, consider using a router table, which may be an easier and safer option.

MORTISE AND TENON JOINTS

In very basic terms, a mortise is a square-sided hole and a tenon is a tongue. There are many variations on the basic mortise and tenon form, which have evolved to answer specific needs. Generally, it is better to cut the mortise first and then the tenon (see opposite).

Cutting a blind mortise with a chisel

Step 1: Take the workpiece, all nicely planed and squared, and use the square to draw guidelines around the wood.

Step 2: Take the mortise gauge and set it directly from the width of the chosen chisel. Use the gauge to run parallel lines from one squared line to the other.

Step 3: With the guidelines in place on one face of the workpiece, clamp the workpiece flat on the bench so that the lines are uppermost.

Step 4: Turn the chisel around so that the bevel is looking towards the middle of the mortise, set the edge a little in from the end of the marked box, hold the chisel so that it is square and vertical, and then give the handle a well-placed blow with a mallet.

Step 5: Rerun the chopping procedure from one end of the mortise to the other, and then use the chisel to clear away the resultant chips.

Step 6: Continue this procedure until the mortise is the required depth, then pare the sides of the mortise to a good finish.

Alternative technique You could clear the bulk of the waste by drilling a line of holes, and then pare the drilled area to create the mortise.

By far the quickest method is to use a mortiser (mortise machine). Mortise cutters are available in standard sizes, so it is best to choose widths to match the cutters or else make multiple cuts.

Blind mortise and tenon

Through-mortise and tenon

Wedged mortise and tenon

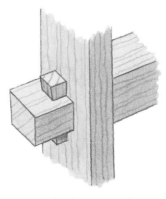

Loose-wedged mortise and tenon

Cutting a tenon with a tenon saw

When cutting a tenon, always take into account the thickness of the saw blade, and make sure that the cut is to the waste side of the guidelines.

Step 1: Use the measure, square and knife to mark in the line of the shoulder. Use the marking or mortise gauge to mark from the shoulder lines up and across the end grain.

Step 2: Secure the workpiece in the vice at an angle of about 60°, then use the tenon saw to cut to the waste side of the gauged lines. Run a cut across the end grain and down to the shoulder line. Reverse the workpiece in the vice and run cuts down to the other shoulder line.

Step 3: Having made four angled cuts, set the wood upright in the vice and saw down to the shoulder line.

Step 4: Finally, set the workpiece hard against a bench hook and saw to the waste side of the shoulder line so that the waste cheeks fall away.

Alternative technique This whole procedure can be done by making a series of side-by-side cuts on a bench saw, sliding compound mitre saw or radial-arm saw. It will help to make practice cuts on an offcut of the same section as you will be using for the real joint. Small adjustments can make a huge difference to the fit of the joint, so keep testing the fit in the mortise. A length stop or end stop is essential otherwise when you turn the component to cut another side of the tenon, the cuts will not line up.

A router table is also capable of cutting tenons. Use a straight cutter and the sliding guide to feed the work at 90° to the fence (or at another angle as necessary).

REBATE JOINTS

The rebate joint, sometimes known as a lap joint, is formed by sitting the end of one board in the stepped rebate of another. It is one step on from a butt joint, in that most of the end grain is hidden from view.

Cutting a cross-grain rebate with a fillister rebate plane

Step 1: Turn the metal spur around so that it is in the "down" cutting position, with the flat face of the spur flush with the flat side of the plane.

Step 2: Set the fence and the depth stop to the size of the rebate.

Step 3: Clamp the workpiece to the bench so that the end to be worked is overhanging. Clamp a piece of waste to the run-off side of the wood, so that the plane can run through without splitting the grain.

Step 4: Hold the plane so that it is level and pressed hard up against the wood, at a point near the far side of the board, and make one well-considered cut. Continue back along the wood.

Step 5: Continue until the shavings stop coming and the depth stop reaches the surface of the wood.

Alternative technique A basic rebate joint can be worked with a router. Fit the router with a straight cutter that is wider than the rebate, adjust the side fence and make a series of deeper and deeper cuts. If the workpiece is too narrow to use the fence (there is not enough for the fence to run against) you can fix scrap wood either side of the workpiece to provide an edge for the fence to run against or, better still, use a router table with the workpiece held against the sliding guide.

Single-sided dovetail housing

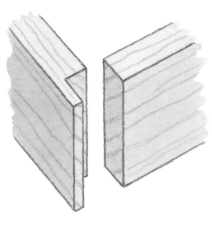

Lap (rebate) joint

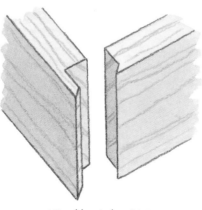

Mitred lap (rebate) joint

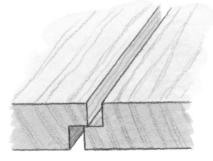

Rebated shiplap

Cutting a hand-worked rebated shiplap

A rebated shiplap is made from two identical rebates or laps, which are aligned to make a flush board.

Step 1: Take the workpiece, all planed and square, and secure it to the bench. If the workpiece is very narrow, you might have to clamp one end and then work the other, and then turn about, or you could pin it in place and settle for filling the pinholes.

Step 2: Measure out the width of the rebate – let's say that it is 15 mm (⅝ in) wide and 10 mm (⅜ in) deep. Pin or clamp a thin batten strip to the workpiece, setting it 15 mm (⅝ in) from the edge of the wood.

Step 3: Take your finely tuned wooden rebate plane, set it flat and hard against the guide strip, and start with the end furthest away from you. Continue making cuts, all the while backing along the wood.

Alternative technique A fillister rebate plane is a very good option for working cross-grain rebates and rebates along the grain, in that it has an integral guide fence and depth gauge. All you do is set the fence and stop, and cut until the stop brings you to a halt.

A quicker way to make this joint is to use a router (or router table if you are using short or small pieces). Practise setting the router using an offcut of the same dimensions as the finished piece. Use the sliding parallel fence guide on the router to set the width of the shiplap. If the rebate is to be wide or deep, either use a large router and large cutter, or make multiple passes, resetting the depth or fence position and removing more wood each time.

HALVING JOINTS

Halving joints, used in the main for creating framed structures, are identical paired half-laps that are designed to notch together.

Cutting a cross-halving or centre-lap

Step 1: One component part at a time, use a ruler, knife and square to establish and draw out the position and shape of the joint. Run the two parallel lines across one face and down both edges.

Step 2: Take a gauge and run lines along the edges, equally dividing the thickness of the wood and linking the parallel lines as they appear on the edges.

Step 3: Set the workpiece on the bench hook and use a tenon saw to make a series of side-by-side cuts across the waste. Make sure that the cuts stop just short of the gauged line.

Step 4: Clear the bulk of the sawn waste with a chisel and then tidy up with the chisel, or better still a small shoulder or rebate plane.

Alternative technique If you are faced with making a lot of identical joints, you could use the router with a jig. Make the jig, set the workpiece in place and clear the waste with a series of shallow overlapping passes.

Another way would be to use a router table; use the sliding guide (you may need to remove the parallel fence) to feed the wood at 90° to the cutter (or at the appropriate angle).

A sliding compound mitre saw, radial-arm saw or table saw can all be used to cut cross-halving joints; make repeated saw cuts, side by side, each slightly overlapping the last, to remove the waste.

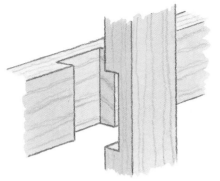

Cross-halving

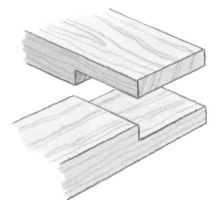

Half-lap

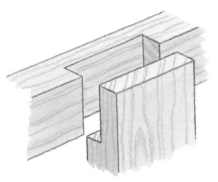

T-halving joint

Dovetail halving joint

Corner halving joints

Corner halving joints, sometimes called end laps, are one of the primary ways of creating a corner joint. This joint is not very strong, but it is fine where the joint is going to be further screwed or bolted, or perhaps strengthened with a sheet of board. Other ways of reinforcing the joint would be to use one or more concealed fluted dowels or drill right through the joint and glue a dowel in place; when the glue is dry, shave the ends of the dowel flush.

Cutting a corner halving on a bandsaw

Step 1: Take the workpiece, all planed and square, and use a ruler, knife and square to mark in the shoulder line. Run the ends of the shoulder line halfway down each edge, and then use a gauge to link the edge lines with a line that runs around the end.

Step 2: With the thickness neatly halved, take a tenon saw and run a cut down to the waste side of the shoulder lines – so that it stops just short of the gauged line.

Step 3: Set the fence and stop on the bandsaw, set the workpiece on edge, and then slide the workpiece hard against the fence and up to the stop to make the cut. Clean up with a shoulder or bullnose plane.

Alternative technique If you are working a large number of identical joints, the bandsaw is a very swift and easy option. The quality of the joint will depend upon the precise position of the stop and the fence.

For more accurate cutting you can use the same techniques as for the cross-halving (router, router table, sliding compound mitre saw, radial-arm saw or table saw.

DOVETAIL JOINTS

Dovetails are winners: they are strong and they look good. The ability to cut dovetails is considered to be the hallmark of fine woodworking.

The angle used for making a dovetail joint varies, depending on whether you are using hardwood or softwood. The angle is calculated by drawing out a slope in the proportions of 1:8 for hardwood, or 1:6 for softwood, or 1:7 for a mix. Draw a rectangle 1 unit wide and 8 units long, and a diagonal line running from one corner to the opposite corner is the dovetail angle. Copy this angle with a sliding bevel and use that when marking out the pins and tails. Alternatively, you can purchase dovetail "squares" or make your own templates.

Making a through-dovetail with a bevel-edged chisel

If you really want to test your woodworking skills, cutting dovetails by hand is going to be an enjoyable challenge. There are lots of ways to do it; here is one of them.

Step 1: Set out the shape of the tails, and shade in the areas that need to be cut away. Use a dovetail saw to cut down to the waste side of every tail. Use the saw to clear the half-pin waste.

Step 2: Use a coping saw to remove the waste from between the tails.

Step 3: Set the workpiece flat on the bench and use a bevel-edged chisel to pare back to the lines.

Step 4: To cut the pins, use the knife to transfer the shape of the tails to the ends of the "pins" board. Square the lines down to the gauged shoulder line, and then saw and pare as already described.

Alternative technique Use a dovetail jig (described opposite).

Through-dovetail

Mitred dovetail joint

Bevelled (compound) dovetail

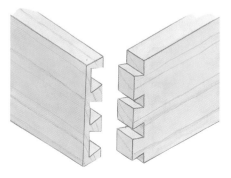

Lapped (stopped or drawer) dovetail

Cutting a drawer dovetail with a chisel

The drawer dovetail is also known as a secret dovetail, or a half-blind dovetail.

Step 1: Set out the tails and cut them out in exactly the way described for the common through-dovetail.

Step 2: Gauge lines on the inside of the drawer front and on the end grain – lines that match the thickness of the drawer sides.

Step 3: Having cut the open tails on the drawer sides, use them to set out the shape of the pins on the inside ends of the drawer front. Use a pencil to carefully shade in the areas that need to be cut away.

Step 4: Use a fine-toothed saw to run cuts slightly to the waste side of the drawn lines – so that they run at an angle from the end grain down towards the drawn shoulder line that you see on the inside of the drawer front.

Step 5: Clamp the drawer front flat on the bench, so that the inside face is uppermost. Use a small chisel to clear the waste and pare down to the lines.

Alternative techniques There are many dovetail-cutting jigs on the market, the majority of which are designed to be used with a router fitted with a dovetail cutter. It is normal for the two pieces to be joined to be held in the jig and the pins and tails cut at the same time; metal "fingers" in the jig guide the router in a series of in-and-out cuts. The great benefit of these jigs is that they negate the marking-out stage, speed up the cutting and produce consistently accurate results. The disadvantages are that they are not suited to cutting fine joints and occasionally the edges of the joint will break out, especially if you are working too fast or if the cutter has become dull.

Sliding slip-feather dovetail tongues

Dovetail tongues are a functional-come-decorative feature, which are used to join two members end to end.

Step 1: Set out the shape of the housing on the end on the workpiece (two boards) so that you can see the characteristic dovetail shape on the end edge of the workpiece.

Step 2: Fit the router with a straight cutter and cut a groove to clear the bulk of the waste, and then follow up with an appropriate dovetail bit.

Step 3: When you have cut the housings, lay out the dovetail shape on the edge of a third piece of wood, and cut the tongue.

Step 4: Set the two boards end to end, and modify the tongue until it is a perfect sliding fit.

Butterfly keys

A butterfly key is two joined dovetail forms, to fit into a shallow recess.

Step 1: Mark out a butterfly key using a try square, ruler, bevel gauge and knife. The grain must run lengthways to prevent snapping. The size and thickness of the key depend on the joint. Use the same wood or a contrasting one.

Step 2: Cut out the butterfly key on the bandsaw, tenon saw or dovetail saw. Trim to a finished shape using a chisel.

Step 3: Set a butterfly on the joint to be reinforced and decorated, and scribe around it with a fine-pointed scalpel.

Step 4: Use a chisel to chop in the outline and to cut out a butterfly-shaped recess. Aim for a tight push-fit.

Step 5: Glue the key in place and plane to a flush finish.

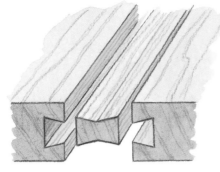

Sliding slip-feather

Butterfly key

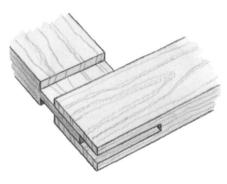

Corner bridle joint

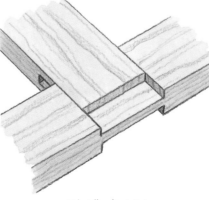

T-bridle slip joint

BRIDLE JOINTS

Bridle joints, also called slip joints, and open-slot mortises, are a sort of evolutionary step between a lap or halving joint and a mortise and tenon.

Making a corner bridle with a chisel and saw

The corner bridle is made up of a tenon and an open-ended mortise.

Step 1: To make the tenon, see page 77.

Step 2: To make the slotted mortise, mark out the wood exactly as you would for the tenon. You will use much the same procedures as for cutting a tenon, but this time you will leave the two side cheeks in place and go on to use the tenon saw and the coping saw to cut away the centre area of waste.

Step 3: Use a chisel to skim the joint to a good fit.

T-bridle slip joint

A very useful joint for a simple flat frame.

Step 1: Cut a slotted mortise as described for the corner bridle joint.

Step 2: To cut the central tenon (or you might say the double lap) use a ruler, knife and square to run the two parallel shoulder lines around all sides and edges of the workpiece.

Step 3: Take a gauge and divide the thickness of the wood into thirds, with lines that link the shoulder lines.

Step 4: Set the workpiece on the bench hook. Use a tenon saw to make a series of side-by-side cuts across the waste.

Step 5: Clear the bulk of the sawn waste with a chisel, and then tidy up with a small shoulder plane.

FIXINGS

The range of fixings and fittings is so huge, and some of the applications so specific, that it can be hard to know where to start when trying to choose a fixing that is appropriate for the task in hand. Here is an outline of the products on the market; see page 69 for nails, pins and screws.

NUTS, BOLTS, THREADED INSERTS AND WASHERS

- **Threaded rod** – Used in conjunction with various secondary fixings, and tends to be used for large-scale knock-down constructions such as beds, cupboards and chairs.

- **Screw socket** – Metal and plastic screw sockets are used in conjunction with man-made boards. The socket is screwed into a hole to provide a captured thread for a bolt.

- **Lock nut** – Lock nuts are used when you want a nut to stay put even when you have withdrawn the bolt.

- **Washer** – Used (in conjunction with nuts and bolts) behind the bolt head or nut to spread the forces, and to prevent the head or nut from damaging the wood.

- **Wing nut** – These are used in situations where there is a likelihood that you will want to disassemble or in some way ease a structure, as with beds and garden furniture.

- **Dome-headed nut** – Designed to be on view. Suitable only for specific situations where you can use set bolt lengths.

- **Cabinet connector** – For use when you want to draw two adjoining structures together – as with two side-by-side cupboards on a wall.

- **Pronged T-nut** – A nut with prongs on one side – it will stay put even when you have removed the bolt.

- **Bolt and barrel nut** – A good option for frame constructions, when you don't want or need to make

Threaded rod

Insert nut

Nylon lock nut

Penny washer

Wing nut

Cross-dowel

Cabinet screw

traditional joints or when you want to make a knock-down construction. The barrel is dropped into one hole, the threaded bolt passed through the joint and into the barrel, and then the bolt is tightened up. The fixing is more or less hidden from view.

- **Block joint** – The block consists of two plastic blocks that fit together. You screw one block to each component part, and then tighten up an integral bolt to draw the two parts together. These joints are great for general DIY work.

CAM-DOWEL FIXINGS

Cam-dowels are ingenious. They consist of two metal components: a screw dowel and a circular cam. You screw the screw dowel into one part, drill a hole and fit a cam into the other part; then slide the two parts together until they locate and turn the cam to lock the parts together. Cam-dowels are very useful fittings.

Expansion plate

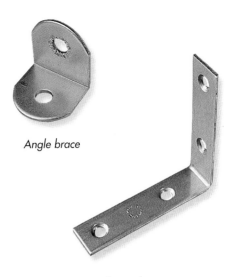

Angle brace

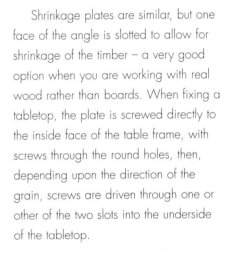

Corner brace

Dowel (cam-dowel fixing)

Cam (cam-dowel fixing)

BRACKETS

Right-angled metal plates are designed to be used in situations when you want to join one part to another at right angles. They are very useful for general DIY work, when you are working with sheet material, such as when making cupboards or pieces of utility furniture.

Shrinkage plates are similar, but one face of the angle is slotted to allow for shrinkage of the timber – a very good option when you are working with real wood rather than boards. When fixing a tabletop, the plate is screwed directly to the inside face of the table frame, with screws through the round holes, then, depending upon the direction of the grain, screws are driven through one or other of the two slots into the underside of the tabletop.

WALL FIXINGS

These plastic fixings can be used in all sorts of item-to-wall situations, such as cupboards on solid walls, cupboards on hollow plaster walls, or frames and shelves on walls. The fixings are generally designed to be used in specific situations with set screw sizes. Choose one that perfectly suits your needs.

STAPLES

Staples (fired in a staple gun) are good for all manner of temporary fixings, when you want to hold or locate a small part while it is being glued or pinned.

Cam-dowel fixings are suited to modern furniture, especially knock-down designs.

FURNITURE HARDWARE

Always buy the very best quality of furniture hardware: solid brassware for furniture, steel hinges for heavy doors, galvanized and plated fixings for exterior work, and so on. There's no sense in making a piece of quality woodwork and then spoiling it with the wrong type of hinge, or a screw that's a poor fit.

HINGES AND STAYS

- **Piano hinge** – Generally used in furniture-making situations where you need a strong but decorative hinge.
- **Brass butt hinge** – Solid brass butt hinges are perfect when you want to fit a top-quality flush hinge on furniture. They come in a good range of widths and lengths.
- **Zinc-plated butt hinge** – A steel hinge that is good for quality DIY work.
- **European-style concealed hinge** – The perfect choice for a cupboard made from man-made board.
- **Strap hinge** – The traditional strap hinge (painted or galvanized) is designed for outside use such as on sheds and gates.

CATCHES, LOCKS AND BOLTS

There are catches, locks and bolts for every situation: brass cabinet locks for small pieces of fine furniture, flap locks for bureaus, ball catches for small doors, roller catches for kitchen furniture, and so on. Spend time at the design stage identifying the item that is best going to suit your needs. Do you want a degree of security? Do you want, say, a cupboard door to open and close at a touch? Do you want to replace a traditional fitting?

There are some very clever touch latches – all you do is push the door to close it, and then give a second push to open it – a really good option for flush doors in situations where you want all the workings hidden from view.

Choose from plastic, steel, brass etc. according to the intended purpose. For example, a sliding brass bolt is just the thing for a piece of furniture or an interior fitting, but it would be out of place on a garden shed. Good, solid latches are just the thing for sheds, but they also look right inside the house when you are trying to create a period or rustic feel, as with latch and catch doors, and tongue-and-groove kitchen furniture.

To sum up, think carefully about functional aspects such as strength, weight, weather resistance, security; and then start thinking about finish and decorative suitability.

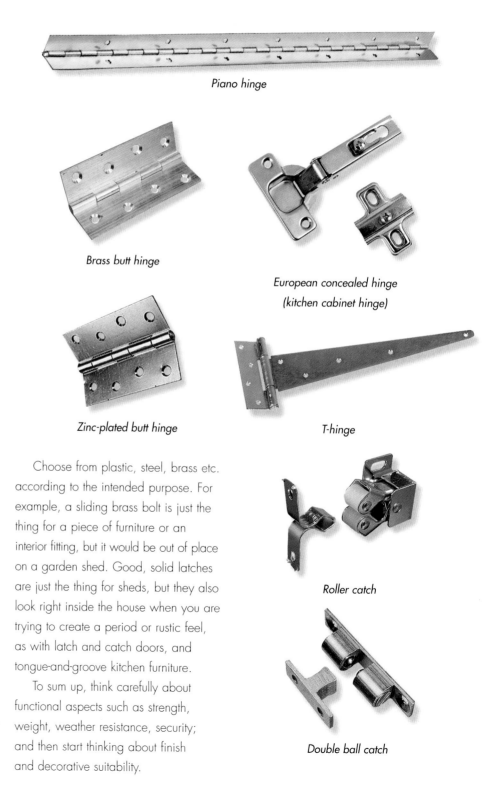

Piano hinge

Brass butt hinge

European concealed hinge (kitchen cabinet hinge)

Zinc-plated butt hinge

T-hinge

Roller catch

Double ball catch

DRAWER RUNNERS

These very useful steel and nylon runners are designed for knock-down cabinets. You screw one part to the frame, the other part to the drawer, and then locate the two. The way the little wheels or rollers run in the tracks makes for a very smooth sliding action.

As with many of these high-tech fittings, the trick is being able to select just the right tracks to suit your needs. For example, there are trigger-release, low-noise adjustable tracks for heavy drawers, tracks for self-closing drawers, runners to fit on the bottom rather than the side of drawers, and so on. It is best to visit a supplier and see just how the various runners are fitted.

HANDLES

Handles must be functional – just the right shape to fit your hand, the right scale to suit the item, safe, secure and well fitted. They are also design features. You have to bring function and form together. Look at the handles on offer, narrow them down to those that suit your functional needs, then think about design.

CASTORS AND WHEELS

There are castors and wheels to suit every woodworking scenario – reproduction castors for antique furniture, locking castors for very heavy utility items, soft wheels for toys, and so on. Castors and wheels must be safe, strong and up to the task.

HIGH-TECH HARDWARE

The range of high-tech hardware is truly amazing. For example, you can now fit your front door with a digital lock that you can program so it will accept your fingertip profile rather than a key. Be open-minded and explore the potential of what is on offer.

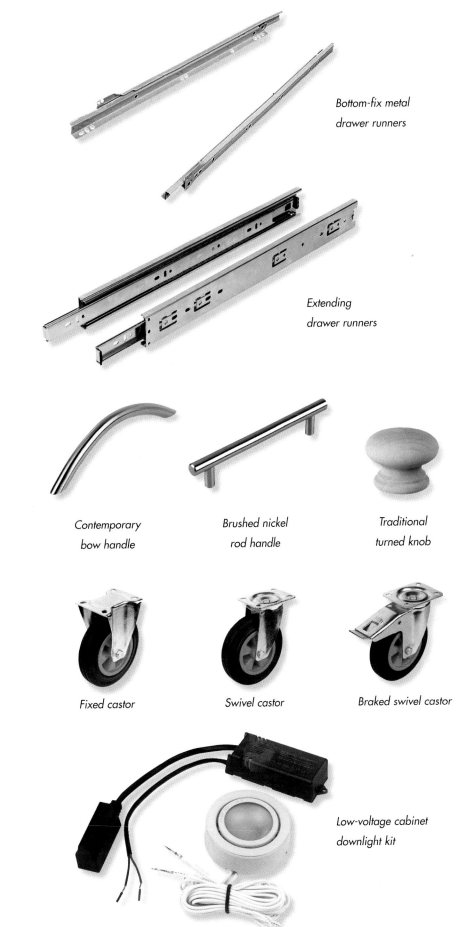

Bottom-fix metal drawer runners

Extending drawer runners

Contemporary bow handle

Brushed nickel rod handle

Traditional turned knob

Fixed castor

Swivel castor

Braked swivel castor

Low-voltage cabinet downlight kit

VENEERING AND INLAYING

These traditional crafts involve covering or in some way embellishing common woods with exotic woods in an attempt either to make the common wood look like a solid slab of exotic wood, and/or to create a pictorial or decorative effect. These procedures are now being used to enhance man-made boards.

EQUIPMENT

Apart from the basic tools that most woodworkers already have, veneering and inlaying require a couple of dedicated thin-bladed saws, a large metal hammer for pressing and compacting the veneers, a glue pot for making animal glues, and a small electric vacuum press.

Veneer saw

Veneer hammer

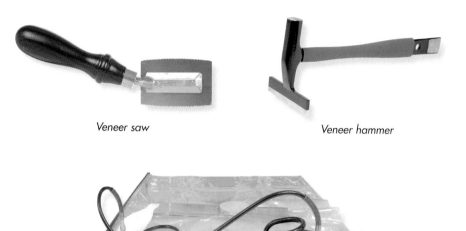

Vacuum bag press

STICKING DOWN SINGLE SHEETS

The traditional method involves applying hot animal glue to both the ground and the veneer, and then setting them together and applying a smoothing pressure with your hands and the hammer. This method is good for large pieces of furniture and for difficult curl or burr veneers.

Alternatively, the modern technique involves sandwiching a sheet of glue film between the veneer and the ground, and applying pressure with an electric iron.

Electric glue bucket for heating glue

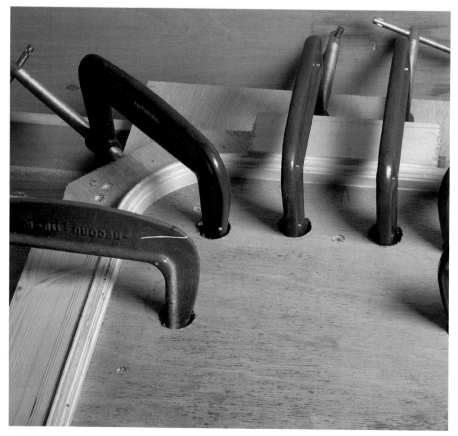

Stiff boards and numerous clamps can be used to glue veneers to flat pieces of wood.

JOINING PIECES OF VENEER AND USING CLAMPS

Set the pieces of veneer together so that the edges are slightly overlapped, and then use a knife or saw to cut through the double thickness so that you achieve a perfect edge-to-edge join. Pin the pieces to a board so that the best face is uppermost, and run a piece of veneer tape down the join.

Brush PVA adhesive on the ground or baseboard, and set the veneer in place with the tape uppermost. Sandwich the whole works between two pieces of plastic sheet, then two pads of newspaper or felt, and finally two cauls or boards. Clamp up, wait for twenty-four hours, then remove the workpiece, peel off the tape, and prepare as with any other surface.

MARQUETRY, PARQUETRY AND INLAYING

Marquetry – Marquetry is the craft of creating a picture, pattern or design from a panel of variously coloured veneers. The picture is then stuck to the surface of a panel, or to some part of a piece of furniture.

Parquetry – Parquetry involves creating a geometrical repeat or a tessellating pattern that can be used decoratively to enhance just about anything from a floor to a piece of furniture. Sometimes described as "veneer patchwork".

Inlaying – Marquetry and parquetry are concerned with applying exotic woods to the surface of a workpiece; inlaying involves recessing and setting exotic woods and various other materials into the background, so that the design features some part of the background.

Marquetry by Paul Dean.

Ready-made inlay "banding" is recessed into routed grooves, glued and taped in position.

WOODCARVING

Woodcarving is one of those crafts where age-old techniques and tools have survived intact. Although there are now electric power gouges, a carver basically works with a collection of chisels, gouges, knives, a bench with a vice or stand, and a carefully chosen block or slab of wood.

CARVING EQUIPMENT

To start with, get yourself a stout bench with a vice or clamp, a small range of top-quality gouges, a couple of knives and a mallet. Buy other tools when you are faced with a specific technical problem, such as carving a deep hole or an unusual curve – then you will know precisely what type, size and shape of tool you need to complete the task. In this way, you will finish up with a kit where each and every tool will have been chosen with knowledge and care.

WOOD CHOICE

Prepared carving blanks (American basswood, also known as lime)

Start with an easy-to-carve, bland wood such as lime or jelutong, then try more challenging woods such as oak and yew. Some grainy, knotty woods are exciting and rewarding to carve, but the easiest option to begin with is to go for straight-grained, knot-free hardwoods.

You could also keep a lookout for wood on riverbanks and beaches, or use old packing cases and bits of old furniture, learning what works by trial and error.

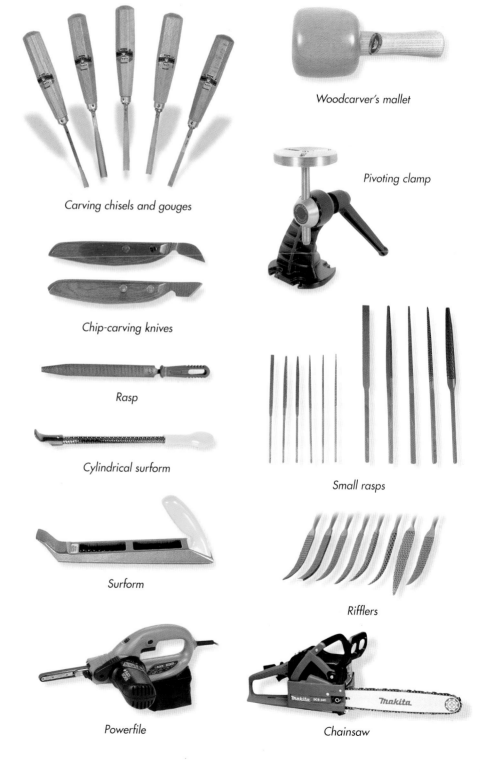

Carving chisels and gouges

Woodcarver's mallet

Pivoting clamp

Chip-carving knives

Rasp

Cylindrical surform

Small rasps

Surform

Rifflers

Powerfile

Chainsaw

Fine relief carving.

RELIEF CARVING

Relief woodcarving includes every type of flat or semi-flat carving. In order of complexity, starting with the simplest, there is what used to be called "primitive" relief (designs scratched on a surface); incised lines that cut slightly deeper into a surface; chip-carved designs that pattern a surface with little knife-worked pockets; naive, folk-art whittled designs in a low relief, which are used to pattern a surface; low-relief designs that wrap around more complex forms, such as a three-dimensional bowl surface-decorated with low-relief designs; and high-relief

Phoenix Rising; oak with wax finish by Chris Pye.

designs that stand up from the surface of the wood – ranging from stylized motifs such as early American sunflower designs through to English medieval misericord-type reliefs that are so deeply undercut and modelled that they are almost three-dimensionally carved in the round.

The order of work for carving an item such as an oak leaf in low relief is as follows. Choose a slab of wood such as lime, transfer the design to the surface of the wood, and use a knife or V-tool to cut a V-section trench around the whole design. Lower the wood to the waste side of the trench so that the leaf is left standing in high relief – like a plateau – and then model the surface details so the leaf has all the undulations, veins and textures of a real leaf. And of course, if you go on to deeply undercut and model the leaf, you will gradually reach a point where there is a blurring of definition as to whether the leaf is relief-carved or carved in the round.

CARVING IN THE ROUND

A carving in the round is defined as a carving that is worked so that it becomes a three-dimensional form that can be viewed from all sides. For example, a freestanding figure or a realistic interpretation of an apple would be described as carved in the round. In-the-round carvings can be realistic or abstract – as long as they can be seen and viewed from all sides.

Traditionally, carving in the round was thought to be the zenith of woodcarving. If you could carve a figure or flower that fooled the eye into believing it was real, you were a master carver. Apprentices began by carving incised lines, then low reliefs, then high reliefs, and finally learned to carve in the round. In this way, they gradually increased their expertise and craft confidence to the point where they were considered to be master carvers.

A fantastic carved and painted horse by Erve Moninger.

WOODTURNING

Woodturning involves cutting and shaping a piece of wood with gouge- and chisel-like tools while it is being spun on a lathe. The workpiece is held between centres, mounted on a faceplate, or held in a chuck – to produce symmetrically circular (as seen centre-on) spindles, discs, bowls and spheres.

WOODTURNING EQUIPMENT

A lathe is like no other woodworking machine. Beginners often opt for the cheapest lathe, thinking that they can upgrade later. When things go wrong, the beginner doesn't know that this has nothing to do with skill level or effort, but is down to the lathe.

So the best advice is to attend a short course, and then buy top-quality tools and equipment. In essence, you need a lathe complete with faceplates, inside and outside callipers, and a range a scrapers, chisels and gouges.

Bowl-turning rest

Chuck

Lathe

Inside callipers

Outside callipers

A Banksia nut turning

Prepared woodturning blanks

1 Domed scraper for inside bowls etc.
2 Skew chisel for smoothing spindles
3 Spindle gouge for general shaping
4 Larger spindle gouge
5 Parting tool for cutting through the turning

WOOD CHOICE

Almost any wood can be turned, but it is best to start with tried and trusted even-grained native varieties such as lime, beech, sycamore, maple, box and cherry. Try other varieties in due course, but be aware that some exotic woods produce potentially toxic dust.

Chris Pye's Tibetan-style stupas in ash with a wax finish.

Segmented vessel by Kevin Neelley.

TURNING BETWEEN CENTRES

This is the procedure of turning items such as spindles and cylinders with the workpiece held between two points, namely the headstock and the tailstock centre. The maximum size of the workpiece is governed by the horizontal distance between the headstock and tailstock, and the vertical distance or "swing" between the centre of spin and the top of the lathe bed or tool rest.

The tool (scraper, chisel or gouge) is held in both hands and set down on the tool rest, and then the tool is braced and advanced until the cutting edge comes into contact with the spinning wood. The type of wood, the rate of spin, and the angle of cut are all significant factors.

FACEPLATE TURNING

Discs, bowls, plates and dishes are generally turned on a faceplate. The workpiece (a slab or blank) is screwed to the faceplate, then the faceplate is mounted on the headstock, either "inboard" over the bed of the lathe, or "outboard" – depending upon your needs and the type and size of the lathe.

Record-breaking faceplate turning!

The tool rest is positioned so that work can be approached face-on. A chuck is used in much the same way as a faceplate, the only difference being that the workpiece is held in jaws rather than being screwed.

SEGMENTED TURNING

Segmented turnings are created by variously cutting and laminating the basic slab or length of wood before it is ever mounted on the lathe. At its simplest, if you take two carefully prepared circular blanks of wood, one light and the other dark, and then glue them together and turn a bowl, the resultant bowl will be in two colours. The more complex the arrangement of the blank, the more complex the finished effect.

Midnight at the Oasis; segmented dish by Raymond Lanham.

Jolly Jumbuck; segmented dish by Raymond Lanham

Segmented vessel by Kevin Neelley.

SANDING AND FINISHING

Finishing is the act of enhancing the appearance of a piece of woodwork by texturing and colouring the surface so that it satisfies various functional, visual and tactile needs. Usually this involves rubbing the wood down with a series of graded abrasives and then sealing it, and sometimes also colouring it.

Aluminium oxide roll

Abrasives

Cloth sanding belts

SANDPAPER AND WIRE WOOL

Traditionally, wood was rubbed down with sandpaper – literally paper coated with a layer of sand. The term is now used generically to describe a whole range of abrasives.

The object of the sanding process is to work through a series of abrasives, from coarse to fine, to achieve a good finish. The type and grade of sandpaper – crushed glass, garnet, aluminium oxide, wire wool – depends upon cost and the type of wood being worked. Wire wool can be dipped in oil or wax and used to achieve a finish with a beautiful sheen.

Wire wool

Drum sanding kit

SANDING TECHNIQUES

Apart from sanding with a power sander, most rubbing down involves a piece of paper held in the hand.

Fold the sandpaper into a pad or wrap it around a suitable block or former. Rub the workpiece in the direction of the grain, being careful that you don't blur delicate details or damage areas of vulnerable soft grain.

An orbital palm sander is ideal for small areas and for rounding over edges and corners.

For smoothing irregular-shaped areas, try sandpaper wrapped around a dowel.

Compressor kit for spraying

Brushes

HVLP spray gun

Compressor for spraying

OIL FINISH

Oils – clear or coloured oil and spirit stains – produce finishes that range from matt to a sheen and a high shine. Depending on the oil and the wood being worked, the oil will, to a greater or lesser extent, stain the wood, fill the grain, and form a protective coating.

After rubbing down the surface of the wood, clean up the dust and debris, and take the workpiece to a dust-free area. Dip a pad of lint-free cotton cloth into the oil and rub it over the surface, sealing the surface. Continue dipping and rubbing until the surface of the wood takes on a finish that suits your needs. You may go on to use a brush or pad, or to wait overnight for the first coat to dry, depending on the oil, the type of wood being worked, and your requirements. There are so many variables that it is always a good idea to test the product and your technique on an offcut before you tackle the workpiece.

BRUSH-APPLIED FINISHES

After rubbing down the surface of the wood, take the workpiece to a dust-free area. Dip the point of the brush into the oil, varnish or lacquer, then brush first with the run of the grain and then across it. When the wood is covered, wait for about ten minutes, then run the brush very lightly in the direction of the grain, being careful not to leave dribbles, bubbles or brush hairs. Be extra careful with edges, using a feather-light stroke from centre to edge, so that the brush leaves the edge with the lightest of light touches.

SPRAYED FINISHES

Spraying involves mixing and thinning a finish according to the manufacturer's directions, and then using a spray gun to create a mist that you can apply to the workpiece.

A sprayed finish is generally more even than one applied with a brush, pad or cloth, but there are important health and safety issues. At least two-thirds of the spray is lost in the air and on surrounding surfaces, so you must install an extractor, and wear protective clothing, a mask, goggles and gloves. Make contact with a professional and ask for hands-on advice and guidance. Modern spraying equipment is now beautifully designed, compact, reliable and reasonably priced.

Set the workpiece on a turntable, turn on the extractor, switch on the spray and create a series of overlapping coats. For best effect, hold and move the spray gun so that the centre of the mist "cone" always hits the workpiece at right angles.

TROUBLESHOOTING

Sooner or later you are going to come up against a woodworking problem – you have made a bad saw cut, your tabletop is dented, the oiled finish is rough, and so on. Have a rest and a cup of tea, and then look at the following tips and start afresh.

PROBLEM	SOLUTION
My local DIY store sells terrible wood. Where can I go for good-quality wood?	Search out a local sawmill. Phone them up, tell them your needs and arrange a visit. Don't be afraid to ask questions, such as how long a piece has been seasoned for, or whether there are cheaper alternatives. The more you know, and the more they think you know, the better the deal.
I have some expensive wood that shows problems – waney edges, dead knots and stains. What can I do?	Draw up full-size patterns for the project and see if you can work around the problems. Plug the dead knots and scrape back the stains before you plane the wood. See if you can turn the wood over for best effect, and/or use it alongside another complementary wood.
My project is made from exotic wood that is difficult to obtain. There seem to be too few pieces: how can I check?	Carefully save every last offcut. Cut all the joints, and then have a complete dry-run assembly. If one of the small components is missing, you can laminate it up from the scrap.
I have a lot of very beautiful wood, but it is in the form of very thin sections. How can I use it to best effect?	You could simply laminate it up to make larger stock. Better still, make a positive design feature of the laminations by sandwiching veneers between the layers. In this way you fool an observer into believing that the laminations were done for decorative effect.
I have cut a through-tenon and it is very loose and sloppy. How can I tighten it?	Glue up the joint. Cut shims or wedges from offcuts, dip them in glue and tap them in on all four sides of the tenon until it fits tightly. Make sure the joint is square. When the glue is cured, plane the face of the joint to a good finish.
I want to cut out ten identical thin plywood shapes on the scroll saw. How do I ensure that they are all identical?	Cut out ten blanks. Transfer the image to one blank. Sandwich the blanks together with double-sided sticky tape, so that the image is on top of the stack. Fit a new blade in the saw and set the tension. Cut out the image, then carefully ease the layers apart and remove the tape.
I've cut a component part to make a box and the on-show end is ragged. How can I fix it?	Take a very sharp and well-tuned block plane and skim the ragged end to give mitred end edges. Do this with all the ends. The mitred ends will appear to be positive design features.
I want to plane across some end grain by hand. How can I stop it splitting off?	Clamp a block of scrap wood hard alongside the workpiece, so that when the plane runs through it splits off the scrap rather than the workpiece. Tune the block plane to make the finest cut, and then work the end grain with the plane held so that it makes a sideways, angled, shearing cut.
I have put a board through the planer, and it is rippled. How can I make good?	Use a well-tuned smoothing plane to shear the peak off the ripples. Use a cabinet scraper to skim the whole surface of the board to a sheen finish. Most fine woodworkers claim that all machine-planed wood needs to be worked with a plane and scraper.

REPAIRS AND RESTORATION

When it comes to making repairs, you have to ensure that you do not detract from the appearance or antique value of a piece and are able to achieve strong, long-lasting repairs. Do not remove antique patina by resanding, and use animal glue to mend old pieces of furniture.

REGLUING JOINTS

Remove all traces of old glue. You cannot put fresh glue over old – it won't survive for any length of time. Animal glue is easy to scrape off; unknown modern glues are less so.

Use animal glue for old furniture that was almost certainly assembled using animal glue. This glue can be softened with warm water or steam, so stubborn joints can be eased apart with the aid of a boiling kettle or wallpaper stripper.

When using clamps, protect the existing finish with protective pads of scrap wood and folded cloth, and remove excess glue with a damp cloth.

REPAIRING BROKEN COMPONENTS

A split component part can be mended if the break is new and roughly follows the grain direction (a lengthwise or diagonal split). Feed thin liquid glue – such as superglue – into the break and then clamp up. Alternatively, inject slightly diluted PVA glue into the split with a syringe.

If a component, such as a tenon, is seriously damaged, remove it from the structure and graft on a new piece of wood; cut off the broken part so that it presents a long angled or scarfed surface, and then laminate a new piece of wood on. The long scarfed face presents a larger surface area for gluing, resulting in a stronger joint.

A component that has snapped right through and is an important structural member should be completely remade.

The challenges of repairing broken antique furniture are to match the timber, the character and finish.

REPRODUCING BROKEN COMPONENTS

The problem with reproducing a broken part is how to match up the wood and the finish. Sometimes it is possible to scavenge a hidden piece from the item being mended, such as a tucked-away batten, block, or reinforcing piece. Other than that, you must spend a lot of time searching out a matching piece of wood. Restoration shops are a good source of materials.

If the components include some woodcarvings, you will need to study the original style and do the following.

- If it has been fretted out, perhaps you should do this by hand to match the saw marks.
- You will need to match the character of the woodcarving.
- Check that your gouges will leave the same size and shape of marks.
- If the original been sanded smooth you will need to do the same.

When matching a finish, it is worth remembering that over a period of years, exposure to sunlight will darken the surface of new wood. Practise on a scrap of new wood to achieve a lighter finish than required. Emulate the knocks and scratches on the original if you wish (see below).

REFINISHING

When repairing a piece of old furniture, it's never a good idea to cut back the old surface. The rule for refinishing is always to do as little as possible. If it is of historical importance, leave the patina (all the dents, scratches, ink stains, old varnish) and do no more than repair broken parts. Leave all the old latches, hinges and catches, or replace them with old ones of the same type. If the piece is so old that it has hand-made nails, or nails that are clenched over the surface so that they are on view, try to leave them untouched. And of course, if the item has true historical value, leave it alone and ask the advice of a specialist.

It is a good idea to use an authentic finish. French polish and other finishing kits are readily available from specialist suppliers. Never apply polyurethane varnish or cellulose lacquer to an old piece of furniture, as it will destroy the patina permanently.

PROJECTS 4

COFFEE TABLE

Express your personal style with this inlaid oak and maple coffee table. You can select from thousands of ready-made inlay motifs (available from mail-order veneer suppliers): floral, modern, traditional and geometric. Choose veneer colours that complement the oak tabletop.

YOU WILL NEED

- Table saw, planer and thicknesser (or buy prepared wood)
- Sliding compound mitre saw
- Mortiser and 10 mm (⅜ in) mortise chisel
- Bandsaw or tenon saw
- Router, circle attachment and 10 mm (⅜ in) straight cutter
- Cordless driver, screwdriver bit, twist bit to suit screws
- Orbital sander, 80-grit and 600-grit sandpaper
- Block plane
- Pencil, ruler, tape measure and try square
- Three sash clamps and four G-clamps
- Wood: see drawing – oak and maple
- Expansion brackets: 4
- Screws to fit expansion brackets
- PVA glue, water and cloth
- Varnish

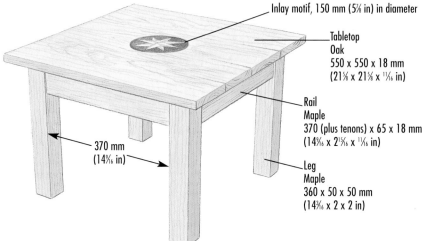

GENERAL VIEW

Inlay motif, 150 mm (5⅞ in) in diameter

Tabletop
Oak
550 x 550 x 18 mm
(21⅝ x 21⅝ x 1¹⁄₁₆ in)

Rail
Maple
370 (plus tenons) x 65 x 18 mm
(14⁹⁄₁₆ x 2¹⁵⁄₁₆ x 1¹⁄₁₆ in)

Leg
Maple
360 x 50 x 50 mm
(14⁹⁄₁₆ x 2 x 2 in)

370 mm
(14⁹⁄₁₆ in)

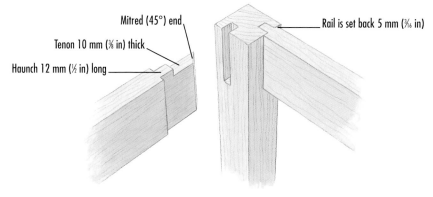

MORTISE AND TENON DETAIL

Rail is set back 5 mm (³⁄₁₆ in)

Mitred (45°) end

Tenon 10 mm (⅜ in) thick

Haunch 12 mm (½ in) long

98

HOW TO MAKE THE COFFEE TABLE

1 Preparing the wood

Cut and plane the legs to the finished size. Prepare the rails, leaving them longer than needed – 460 mm (18⅛ in). Prepare four equal-width boards for the tabletop, leaving them longer than needed – 560 mm (22¹⁄₁₆ in); use the try square to check that the edges are square to the faces.

2 Gluing the tabletop together

Arrange the four boards so the direction of the end-grain growth rings alternates (one curves upward, the next downward etc.) and the colour and grain pattern of adjacent boards blend as much as possible. Label them in order. Practise clamping to check the joints. Glue and clamp (see pages 70–72).

3 Cutting the mortises

Mark the position of the mortises on the legs. Set the mortiser to cut mortises 10 mm (⅜ in) wide and to a depth that is sufficient for the adjacent mortises to meet up inside the leg. Set the depth stop on the mortiser to cut a mortise 12 mm (½ in) deep in the top end of the legs, to take the haunch part of the tenon.

4 Cutting the tenons

Cut the tenons with a compound mitre saw (see page 77 for techniques). Make trial cuts on both sides of the end of a tenon to achieve the correct depth. A waste piece can be used to indicate the position of the blade. Complete the tenon by making repeated overlapping cuts. Cut the haunch with the bandsaw and mitre the ends.

5 Assemble the frame

Check that the joints work and label the parts. Plane off the sharp corners and sand the pieces smooth. Apply varnish (do not varnish the joint areas), lightly sand again and apply a second coat. Prepare wood blocks to protect the workpiece and set the clamps. Glue, clamp and check for squareness.

6 Inlaying the motif

Use the router and circle attachment to cut a recess in the centre of the tabletop for the inlay motif (the veneer should be fractionally proud). Glue and clamp the inlay using four G-clamps: lay several sheets of paper over the inlay, followed by a scrap of thick plywood, before clamping. Sand the inlay flush with the tabletop. Attach the tabletop to the frame with four expansion brackets.

SHAKER HALL MIRROR

This small, wall-hung hallway mirror draws its inspiration from the Shaker tradition. The Shakers were known for their simple, well-crafted furniture characterized by beautiful proportions, "minimalistic" designs and honey-coloured wood.

YOU WILL NEED

- Table saw, planer and thicknesser (or buy prepared wood)
- Sliding compound mitre saw
- Router, router table and straight cutters: 10 mm (⅜ in) and 4 mm (⁵⁄₃₂ in)
- Cordless driver, screwdriver bit, combination bit (drills a counterbored clearance hole and pilot hole) and plug-cutter set to suit No. 8 screws and screwdriver bit
- Crosshead screwdriver
- Pin hammer
- Long-nosed pliers
- Pillar drill, 6 mm (¼ in) and 12 mm (½ in) drill bits
- Orbital sander, 80-grit and 600-grit sandpaper, sanding block
- Block plane
- Pencil, ruler, tape measure, try square
- Two sash clamps and two G-clamps
- Wood: see drawing – pine, plywood, pine egg-shaped details and handle
- Mirror glass: 298 x 228 x 6 mm (11¾ x 9 x ¼ in)
- Corner plates to fix mirror, with screws: 4
- Screws: No.8 cross-headed countersink: 10 x 30 mm (1³⁄₁₆ in)
- Fluted dowels: 20 x 6 mm (¼ in)
- Pins: 8 x 12 mm (½ in)
- Wall-fixing plates, plugs and screws
- PVA glue, water and cloth
- Varnish

GENERAL VIEW

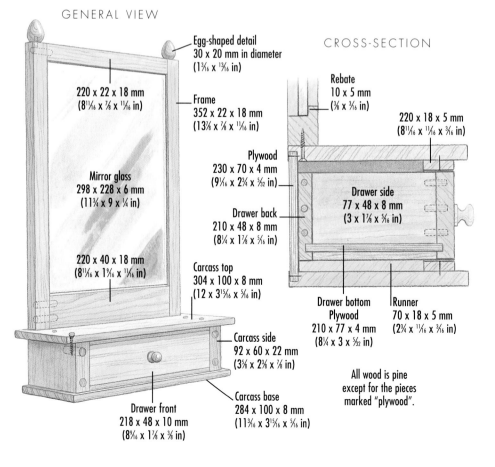

220 x 22 x 18 mm
(8¹¹⁄₁₆ x ⅞ x ¹¹⁄₁₆ in)

Egg-shaped detail
30 x 20 mm in diameter
(1³⁄₁₆ x ¹³⁄₁₆ in)

Frame
352 x 22 x 18 mm
(13⅞ x ⅞ x ¹¹⁄₁₆ in)

Mirror glass
298 x 228 x 6 mm
(11¾ x 9 x ¼ in)

220 x 40 x 18 mm
(8¹¹⁄₁₆ x 1⅝ x ¹¹⁄₁₆ in)

CROSS-SECTION

Rebate
10 x 5 mm
(⅜ x ³⁄₁₆ in)

220 x 18 x 5 mm
(8¹¹⁄₁₆ x ¹¹⁄₁₆ x ³⁄₁₆ in)

Plywood
230 x 70 x 4 mm
(9¹⁄₁₆ x 2¾ x ⁵⁄₃₂ in)

Drawer back
210 x 48 x 8 mm
(8¼ x 1⅞ x ⁵⁄₁₆ in)

Drawer side
77 x 48 x 8 mm
(3 x 1⅞ x ⁵⁄₁₆ in)

Carcass top
304 x 100 x 8 mm
(12 x 3¹⁵⁄₁₆ x ⁵⁄₁₆ in)

Drawer bottom
Plywood
210 x 77 x 4 mm
(8¼ x 3 x ⁵⁄₃₂ in)

Runner
70 x 18 x 5 mm
(2¾ x ¹¹⁄₁₆ x ³⁄₁₆ in)

All wood is pine
except for the pieces
marked "plywood".

Carcass side
92 x 60 x 22 mm
(3⅝ x 2⅜ x ⅞ in)

Carcass base
284 x 100 x 8 mm
(11³⁄₁₆ x 3¹⁵⁄₁₆ x ⁵⁄₁₆ in)

Drawer front
218 x 48 x 10 mm
(8⁹⁄₁₆ x 1⅞ x ⅜ in)

HOW TO MAKE THE SHAKER HALL MIRROR

1 Rebating the frame

Cut and plane all the components to size. Use the router and the 10 mm (⅜ in) straight cutter, set in the router table, to cut rebates in the vertical and horizontal members of the mirror frame for receiving the mirror glass. The rebates in the vertical members should start 15 mm (¹⁹⁄₃₂ in) in from the top end and stop 30 mm (1³⁄₁₆ in) from the bottom end.

2 Assembling the frame

The frame is jointed together using the fluted dowels: one at each of the top corners and two at the bottom corners. Mark out the position of the dowel holes and carefully drill to a depth that is slightly greater than half the length of the dowel. Apply glue to the inside of the dowel holes, insert the dowels, clamp and check that the frame is square.

3 Fixing runners

Cut rebates in the top, base and ends of the carcass to take the plywood back. Mark the position of the runners (strips of wood) and the carcass sides on the top and base of the carcass. Round over the edges and corners of both pieces with the block plane and a piece of sandpaper wrapped around a sanding block. Use glue and pins to fix the runners.

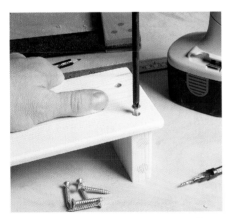

4 Fixing the base to the sides

Drill 12 mm (½ in) holes in the carcass sides and glue the dowels in place, leaving them slightly proud. When dry, plane the dowel ends flush. Mark the positions of screwholes in the base. Drill through the base and into the ends, using the combination bit, and fix with screws.

5 Fixing the top to the frame

Mark the position of the screw-holes in the carcass top. Using the combination bit, drill through the top and into the frame, and fix with screws. Locate the frame and top on the base and sides, and drill through the top and into the sides, again using the combination bit. Fix with screws. Fit the carcass back using pins.

6 Making the drawer

Rout grooves in the drawer components to hold the drawer bottom. Mark and drill holes for the dowel joints at each corner of the drawer. Assemble using glue, one sash clamp and two G-clamps. Plug the screwholes in the top of the carcass, fix the egg-shaped details and drawer handle, sand and varnish. Fit the back of the mirror with the wall-fixing plates and fix to the wall.

ROCKING HORSE

Do your children keep pestering you for a pony? Perhaps this rocking horse will keep them quiet! The design is suitable for six-year-olds, but they must be supervised by an adult when using it. The main challenge for the woodworker is cutting and planing the curved shapes and achieving a smooth rocking motion. The horse could also be painted and decorated in a Wild West theme.

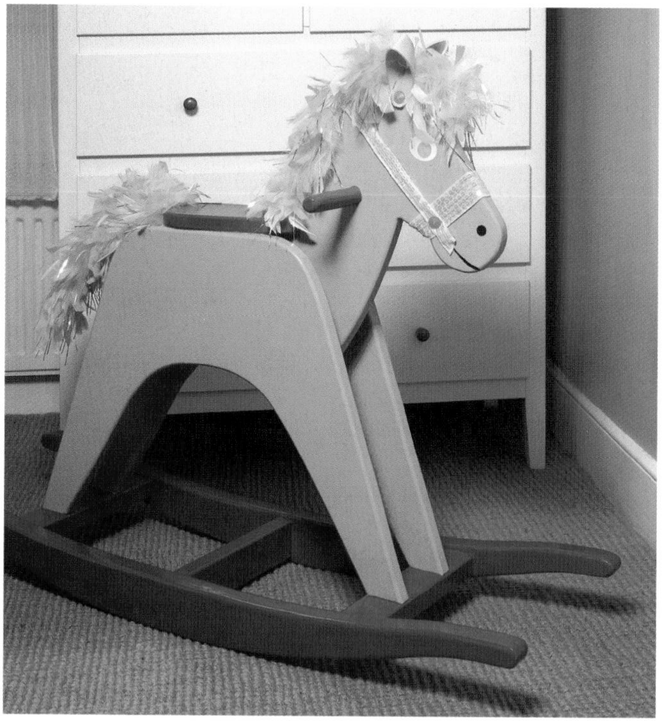

YOU WILL NEED

- Table saw, planer and thicknesser (or buy prepared wood)
- Sliding compound mitre saw
- Mortiser and 12 mm (½ in) mortise chisel
- Bandsaw
- Router, router table, 10 mm (⅜ in) straight cutter and round-over cutter with a guide bearing at the tip
- Cordless driver, screwdriver bit, combination bit (drills a counterbored clearance hole and pilot hole) and plug-cutter set to suit No. 8 screws and screwdriver bit
- Orbital sander, 80-grit and 600-grit sandpaper
- Spokeshave
- Pencil, ruler, tape measure and try square
- Three sash clamps
- Wood: see drawing – pine, plywood and dowelling
- Screws: No. 8 cross-headed countersink: 20 x 40 mm (1 9/16 in)
- PVA glue, water and cloth
- Paint and decorations (feather boa for mane, felt for eyes and sequinned ribbon for bridle)

SIDE VIEW

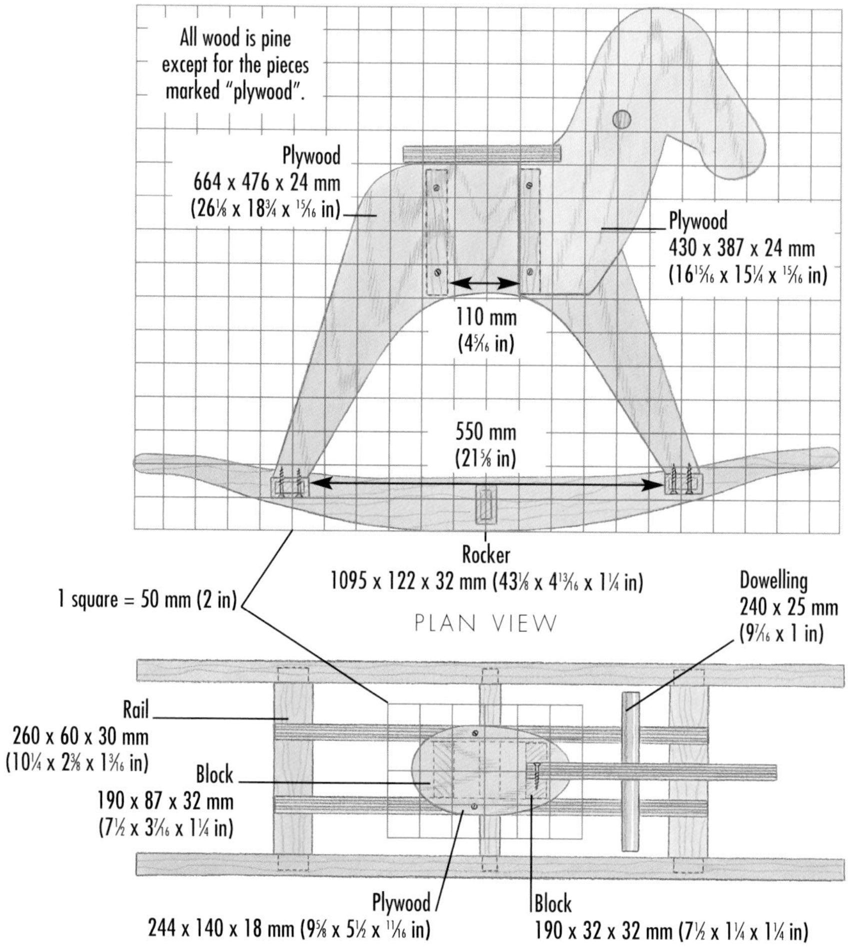
All wood is pine except for the pieces marked "plywood".
Plywood
664 x 476 x 24 mm
(26⅛ x 18¾ x 15/16 in)
Plywood
430 x 387 x 24 mm
(16 15/16 x 15¼ x 15/16 in)
110 mm
(4 5/16 in)
550 mm
(21⅝ in)
Rocker
1095 x 122 x 32 mm (43⅛ x 4 13/16 x 1¼ in)
1 square = 50 mm (2 in)
Dowelling
240 x 25 mm
(9 7/16 x 1 in)
PLAN VIEW
Rail
260 x 60 x 30 mm
(10¼ x 2⅜ x 1 3/16 in)
Block
190 x 87 x 32 mm
(7½ x 3 7/16 x 1¼ in)
Plywood
244 x 140 x 18 mm (9⅝ x 5½ x 11/16 in)
Block
190 x 32 x 32 mm (7½ x 1¼ x 1¼ in)

HOW TO MAKE THE ROCKING HORSE

1 Preparing the wood

Cut and plane all the pine sections to size, allowing extra length for the tenons on both ends of the rails. Draw one half of the shape of a rocker on paper, using a full-size grid to help you plot the outline. Cut out the shape and trace around it on the wood (flip over for the other half).

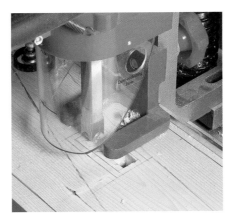

2 Cutting the mortises

Mark the position of the rails and the mortises on the rockers (not yet sawn to shape). Set up the mortiser to cut mortises slightly deeper than the length of the tenons. If the wood is soft, the full depth of the tenon can be cut in one plunge; otherwise, make several plunges, each time raising the cutter in order to clear the waste.

3 Cutting the rockers

Adjust the bandsaw in preparation for cutting out the rockers. Cut to the waste side of the outline, and work slowly and carefully in order to produce a smooth, accurate curve. You will need to make a series of separate small cuts to create the rounded ends. Use the spokeshave to smooth and round over the ends and corners.

4 Cutting the plywood shapes

Mark out the shapes of the plywood components; as before, use a full-size grid to help you plot the shape of the outlines. Cut out the paper pieces and trace around them on the plywood. Cut out on the bandsaw and use the spokeshave to smooth the edges.

5 Cutting the tenons

Use the router, router table and straight cutter to cut the tenons on the ends of the rails. Practise first on a scrap of wood of the same thickness: cut one side, flip it over to cut the other side and test to see if it is a tight fit in the mortises. Assemble the rockers and rails using glue and sash clamps.

6 Assembling the horse

Use the round-over router cutter to round over the edges of the plywood shapes (where exposed). Mark the position of the blocks that join the two sides. Use the combination bit to drill screwholes through the plywood and into the blocks. Assemble the horse and fix to the base. Plug the counterbored holes, sand, paint and decorate.

103

FIDDLEBACK MIRROR

This high-quality mirror frame would look impressive above a fireplace. The simple, modern design incorporates a highly decorative veneer (we have used fiddleback sycamore) and a fine border (stringing) made from dyed boxwood.

YOU WILL NEED

- Table saw, planer and thicknesser (or buy prepared wood)
- Sliding compound mitre saw
- Knife
- Metal straight-edge 1 m (39⅜ in) long
- Router, 10 mm (⅜ in) straight cutter with a guide bearing at the tip, and a 10 mm (⅜ in) straight cutter
- Biscuit jointer and biscuits
- Cordless driver, screwdriver bit and twist bit
- Orbital sander and 600-grit sandpaper
- Pencil, ruler, tape measure and try square
- Six sash clamps, six G-clamps and one frame clamp
- Wood: see drawing – MDF, maple, fiddleback veneer, "balancing" veneer and dyed boxwood stringing
- Scrap plywood and battens
- Mirror glass: 608 x 438 x 6 mm (23¹⁵⁄₁₆ x 17¼ x ¼ in)
- Mirror-fixing plates: 8 with screws
- Wall-mounting plates: 2 with screws
- Veneer pins: 8 x 10 mm (⅜ in)
- PVA glue, water and cloth
- Masking tape
- Varnish

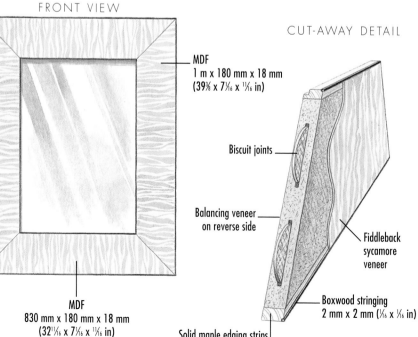

FRONT VIEW

CUT-AWAY DETAIL

MDF
1 m x 180 mm x 18 mm
(39⅜ x 7⁷⁄₁₆ x ¹¹⁄₁₆ in)

Biscuit joints

Balancing veneer
on reverse side

Fiddleback
sycamore
veneer

Boxwood stringing
2 mm x 2 mm (¹⁄₁₆ x ¹⁄₁₆ in)

Solid maple edging strips
10 mm (⅜ in) thick

MDF
830 mm x 180 mm x 18 mm
(32¹¹⁄₁₆ x 7⁷⁄₁₆ x ¹¹⁄₁₆ in)

HOW TO MAKE THE FIDDLEBACK MIRROR

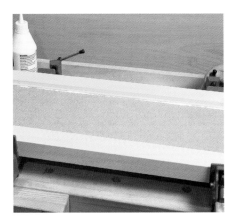

1 Preparing the wood

Cut the MDF into boards 180 mm (7⅟₆ in) wide. Allow 25 mm (1 in) extra length on each piece for wastage. Prepare solid maple strips at least 2 mm (⅟₆ in) wider than the thickness of the MDF and edge the boards with it: glue and clamp the strips, making sure they are centred on the MDF.

2 Routing the edges

Use the router and straight cutter with a bearing tip to cut the edging strips flush with the surface of the MDF. (The bearing follows the surface of the MDF and the cutters extend to the same level as the bearing.) A scrap piece of wood, clamped alongside at the same level, will provide more support for the base of the router.

3 Preparing the veneer

The boards need to be veneered with decorative veneer on one side and a "balancing" veneer on the reverse side. The balancing veneer can be a cheaper species, but the grain must run in the same direction. Without the balancing veneer, the boards will bow as the glue dries and the veneer shrinks. Cut the veneer into pieces about 10 mm (⅜ in) larger than needed all around.

4 Veneering

Cut three pieces of scrap plywood, about 25 mm (1 in) larger all around than the boards. Set up the clamps and practise clamping without glue. Take apart. For each side of the MDF, spread glue, apply the veneer and hold in place with a veneer pin at each end. Stack up the MDF and scrap wood. It is a good idea to include a sheet of paper between each sheet of veneer. Reclamp.

5 Routing the rebates

Once dry, trim the veneer with a knife and sand the edges smooth. Use the router, fitted with the straight cutter and a parallel guide, to cut a 5 x 5 mm (⅜₆ x ⅜₆ in) rebate down one side of the back of each board to take the mirror. Reset the router to cut the smaller rebates on the front sides for the stringing. The stringing should be slightly proud. Glue and tape in position and allow to dry.

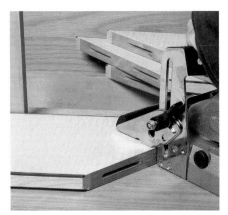

6 Cutting the mitres

Sand the stringing flush with the rest of the board. Set the compound mitre saw for a perfect 45° cut. Practise on a scrap of wood first. Use the biscuit jointer to make corner joints. Glue and assemble, using the frame clamp. When dry, sand and finish. Fit the mirror glass into the back, using the metal fixings to hold it in place. Fit wall-mounting plates to the back of the finished mirror.

BIRD TABLE

This bird table can either hang
from a tree branch, as shown in
the photograph, or be mounted
on a post (the drawing shows
this alternative). The design can
be made out of ready-prepared
pine from your local DIY store.
Finish the wood with colourful
stains and a preservative.

YOU WILL NEED

- Table saw, planer and thicknesser
  (or buy prepared wood)
- Sliding compound mitre saw
- Bandsaw
- Cordless driver, screwdriver bit,
  combination bit (drills a counterbored
  clearance hole and pilot hole) and
  plug-cutter set to suit No. 8 screws
  and screwdriver bit
- Crosshead screwdriver
- Sanding block and 80-grit sandpaper
- Chisel: 25 mm (1 in)
- Pencil, ruler, tape measure, try square
- One fast-clamp
- Paintbrush
- Wood: see drawing – pine
- Screws: No. 8 cross-headed, zinc-
  plated, countersink: 54 x 20 mm
  (1³⁄₁₆ in)
- PVA glue, water and cloth
- Stain and preservative

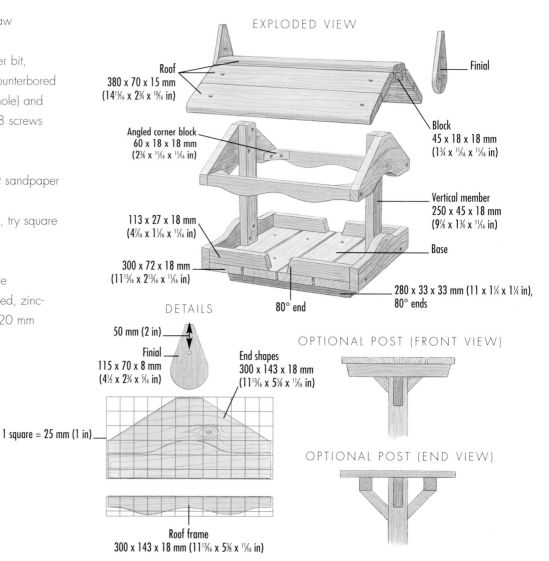

EXPLODED VIEW

Roof
380 x 70 x 15 mm
(14¹⁵⁄₁₆ x 2¾ x ¹⁹⁄₁₆ in)

Finial

Block
45 x 18 x 18 mm
(1¾ x ¹¹⁄₁₆ x ¹¹⁄₁₆ in)

Angled corner block
60 x 18 x 18 mm
(2⅜ x ¹¹⁄₁₆ x ¹¹⁄₁₆ in)

Vertical member
250 x 45 x 18 mm
(9⅞ x 1¾ x ¹¹⁄₁₆ in)

113 x 27 x 18 mm
(4⁷⁄₁₆ x 1¹⁄₁₆ x ¹¹⁄₁₆ in)

Base

300 x 72 x 18 mm
(11¹³⁄₁₆ x 2¹³⁄₁₆ x ¹¹⁄₁₆ in)

280 x 33 x 33 mm (11 x 1¼ x 1¼ in),
80° ends

80° end

DETAILS

50 mm (2 in)

Finial
115 x 70 x 8 mm
(4½ x 2¾ x ⁵⁄₁₆ in)

End shapes
300 x 143 x 18 mm
(11¹³⁄₁₆ x 5⅝ x ¹¹⁄₁₆ in)

1 square = 25 mm (1 in)

OPTIONAL POST (FRONT VIEW)

OPTIONAL POST (END VIEW)

Roof frame
300 x 143 x 18 mm (11¹³⁄₁₆ x 5⅝ x ¹¹⁄₁₆ in)

HOW TO MAKE THE BIRD TABLE

1 Making the base

Purchase all the pine as ready-prepared sections. Buy a little more than you need in case you make a mistake. The whole table is fixed together using screws that are set below the surface of the wood in counterbored holes and then plugged (see step 6). Cut the base pieces to size with the compound mitre saw. Clamp in position, drill holes with the combination bit and screw together.

2 Cutting the end shapes

The curved shapes at each end of the bird table are produced on the bandsaw, as shown above (one cut produces two pieces). Mark out this curved shape using the grid on the drawing as a guide. Set the bandsaw guide and blade guard as low as possible. Use a push-stick to help feed the work through.

3 Assembling the ends

Mark the position of the vertical member on the curved end shapes with a ruler and try square. Use the clamp to hold the wood in the correct position. Check for squareness with the try square before drilling the fixing holes with the combination bit. Place the holes along a diagonal path for added strength. Fix with screws.

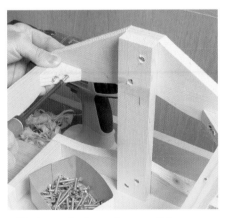

4 Fixing the ends to the base

It is then a simple task to fix the ends to the base you have already made. Position the end, drill fixing holes and screw in place. Repeat for the other end (check that the ends are perpendicular to the base with the try square).

5 Completing the roof frame

Mark out the wavy shapes beneath the roof using the grid on the drawing as a guide. Cut out one on the bandsaw and trace around it to mark the shape of the second piece. Cut angled corner blocks on the compound mitre saw. Note the grain direction of these. Screw the corner blocks to the wavy shapes and complete the roof frame as shown.

6 Fixing the roof

The roof is made from five pieces of pine with a rounded profile (bought ready prepared). Screw the pieces in place. Cut and fix the finials (attached to small blocks). Cut wood plugs to fill the screwholes; glue in place and chisel flush when dry. Sand all edges and corners. Apply stain and preservative. You could also make a post with brackets, as shown in the drawing.

CANDLESTICKS

These candlesticks are made on a lathe, using a combination of woods for decorative effect, and are ideal projects for those new to the craft of turning. The thin candlestick is made from zebrano, which can be purchased from a specialist turning supplier.

YOU WILL NEED

- Table saw, planer and thicknesser (or buy prepared wood)
- Workbench and vice
- Smoothing plane
- Sliding compound mitre saw
- Lathe, roughing-out gouge, skew chisel, parting tool and diamond-point scraper
- Awl
- Compass
- Pencil, ruler and tape measure
- Four G-clamps
- Wood: see drawing – zebrano, beech and oak
- Sandpaper: 80-grit and 600-grit
- Wax polish
- PVA wood glue
- Glass "plate" candleholder: approx. 110 mm (4⁵⁄₁₆ in) in diameter
- Glass tealight-type candleholder: approx. 30 mm (1³⁄₁₆ in) in diameter
- Glue suitable for sticking glass to wood

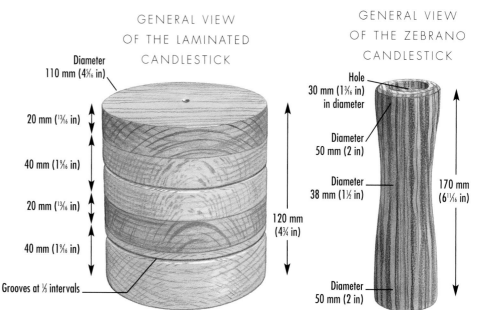

GENERAL VIEW OF THE LAMINATED CANDLESTICK

Diameter 110 mm (4⁵⁄₁₆ in)

20 mm (1³⁄₁₆ in)

40 mm (1⁹⁄₁₆ in)

20 mm (1³⁄₁₆ in)

40 mm (1⁹⁄₁₆ in)

120 mm (4¾ in)

Grooves at ⅓ intervals

GENERAL VIEW OF THE ZEBRANO CANDLESTICK

Hole 30 mm (1³⁄₁₆ in) in diameter

Diameter 50 mm (2 in)

Diameter 38 mm (1½ in)

170 mm (6¹¹⁄₁₆ in)

Diameter 50 mm (2 in)

HOW TO MAKE THE ZEBRANO CANDLESTICK

1 Preparing the wood

Buy a zebrano turning blank from a specialist supplier. Draw diagonals on both ends to establish the centre points. Mark the centre points with the awl. Draw circles on the end, to the correct size, with the compass. Place the blank in the vice and plane off the corners to achieve a rough cylinder shape ready for turning.

2 Turning

Mount the cylindrical blank between the lathe centres and check that it is securely fixed. Wear a dust mask and goggles to protect yourself. Switch on the lathe, and hold the roughing-out gouge firmly against the tool rest at an upward-facing and slanting angle. Raise the handle of the gouge gradually until you feel it "bite".

3 Finishing

Move the gouge left and right to clear the bulk of the waste, then take finer shavings. Stop the lathe now and again to inspect the finish. Use sandpaper (whilst the lathe is turning) to smooth the surface. Mark the end of the candlestick and cut through at that point with the parting tool. Drill hole for candleholder (not to be glued). Finish with wax polish.

HOW TO MAKE THE LAMINATED CANDLESTICK

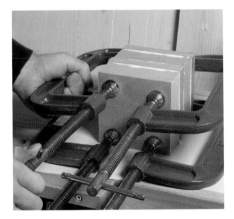

1 Laminating

This candlestick is made from blocks of beech and oak glued together. Cut out the two squares of beech and the two squares of oak with the compound mitre saw. Apply glue to the faces and clamp together using four G-clamps. Note that the grain of each block should run in the same direction. Wipe off the excess glue with a damp cloth.

2 Planing and turning

When dry, remove the clamps and prepare a rough cylinder shape with centre points as described in step 1 above. Mount the cylinder in the lathe, check that it is secure, put on dust mask and goggles, start the lathe and remove the bulk of the waste with the roughing-out gouge. Continue with the skew chisel. Cut the V-section grooves with the diamond-point scraper.

3 Finishing

Use sandpaper (whilst the lathe is turning) to smooth the surface. Stop the lathe now and again to check that there are no pits in the end-grain areas. If there are, use coarse sandpaper to remove them. Finish with fine sandpaper and wax polish. Alternatively, use carnauba wax, which should be applied whilst the lathe is turning. Glue the glass plate to the top of the candlestick.

BEDSIDE TABLE

This bedside table is a companion to the chest of drawers on page 114. It uses the same materials and construction methods. We have used a basic dovetail jig to produce the drawer joints, but you may wish to avoid that expense and use rebate joints like those on the bookcase drawers on page 146.

YOU WILL NEED

- Table saw, planer and thicknesser (or buy prepared wood)
- Sliding compound mitre saw
- Bandsaw
- Spokeshave
- Router, router table, dovetail jig with cutter, 10 mm (⅜ in) and 5 mm (³⁄₁₆ in) straight cutters, and a 10 mm (⅜ in) straight cutter with a guide bearing at the tip
- Pillar drill
- Crosshead screwdrivers
- Cordless driver, screwdriver bit, twist bits to suit cam-dowel fixings and dowels, and countersink bit
- Orbital sander, 80-grit and 600-grit sandpaper, sanding block
- Block plane
- Pencil, ruler, tape measure and try square
- Two sash clamps
- Rubber mallet
- Iron
- Wood: see drawing – oak, oak pre-veneered MDF, oak iron-on veneer edging strip, two oak knobs, pine
- Plastic joining blocks with screws: 4
- Cam-dowel fixings: 20
- Fluted dowels: 8 x 8 mm (⁵⁄₁₆ in)
- Screws: No. 8 cross-headed, zinc-plated, countersink: 8 x 20 mm (1³⁄₁₆ in)
- PVA glue, water and cloth
- Finishing oil

EXPLODED GENERAL VIEW

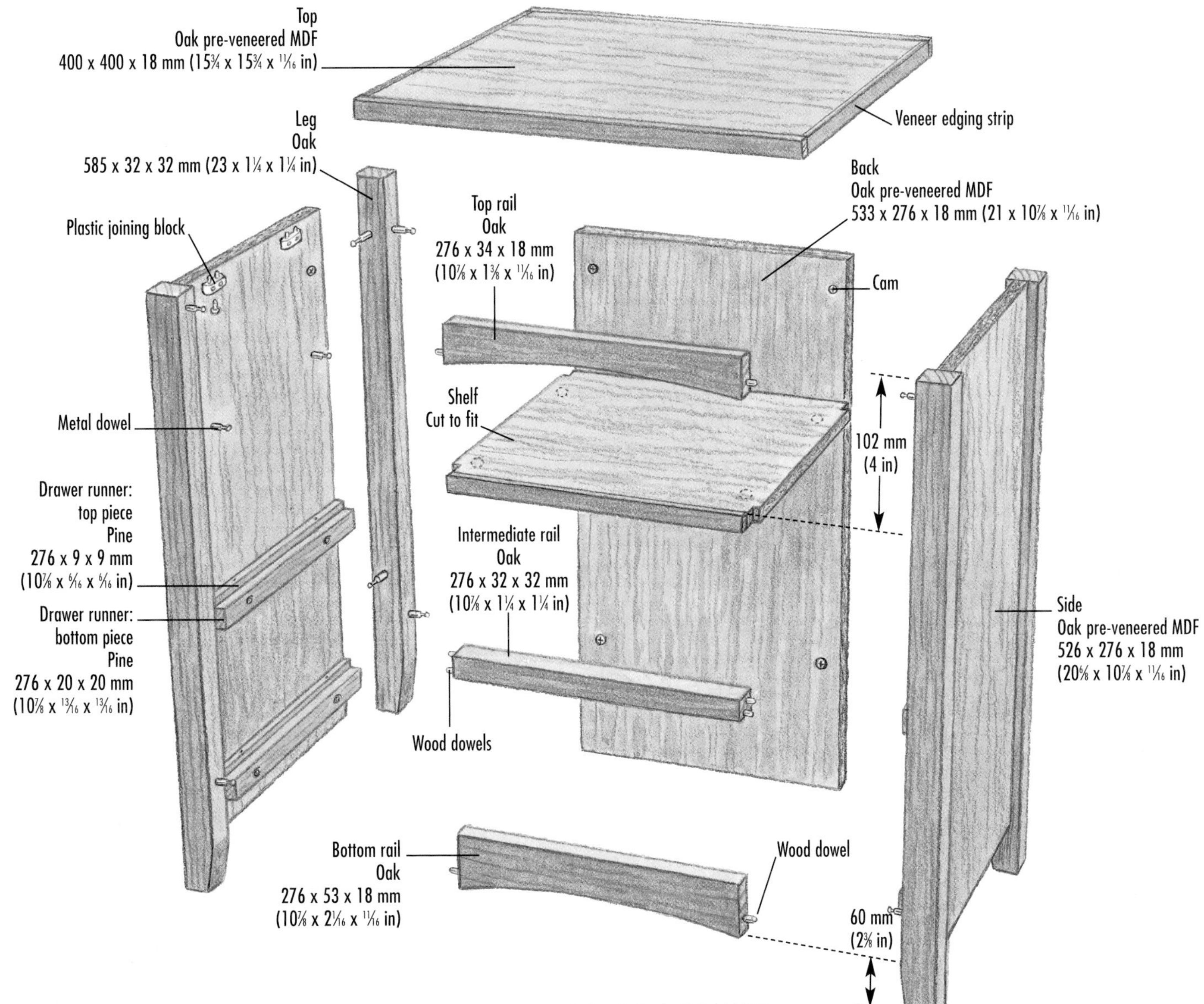
Top
Oak pre-veneered MDF
400 x 400 x 18 mm (15¾ x 15¾ x 11/16 in)
Veneer edging strip
Leg
Oak
585 x 32 x 32 mm (23 x 1¼ x 1¼ in)
Back
Oak pre-veneered MDF
533 x 276 x 18 mm (21 x 10⅞ x 11/16 in)
Plastic joining block
Top rail
Oak
276 x 34 x 18 mm
(10⅞ x 1⅜ x 11/16 in)
Cam
Shelf
Cut to fit
Metal dowel
102 mm
(4 in)
Drawer runner:
top piece
Pine
276 x 9 x 9 mm
(10⅞ x 5/16 x 5/16 in)
Intermediate rail
Oak
276 x 32 x 32 mm
(10⅞ x 1¼ x 1¼ in)
Side
Oak pre-veneered MDF
526 x 276 x 18 mm
(20⅝ x 10⅞ x 11/16 in)
Drawer runner:
bottom piece
Pine
276 x 20 x 20 mm
(10⅞ x 13/16 x 13/16 in)
Wood dowels
Bottom rail
Oak
276 x 53 x 18 mm
(10⅞ x 2⅛ x 11/16 in)
Wood dowel
60 mm
(2⅜ in)

EXPLODED VIEW OF A DRAWER

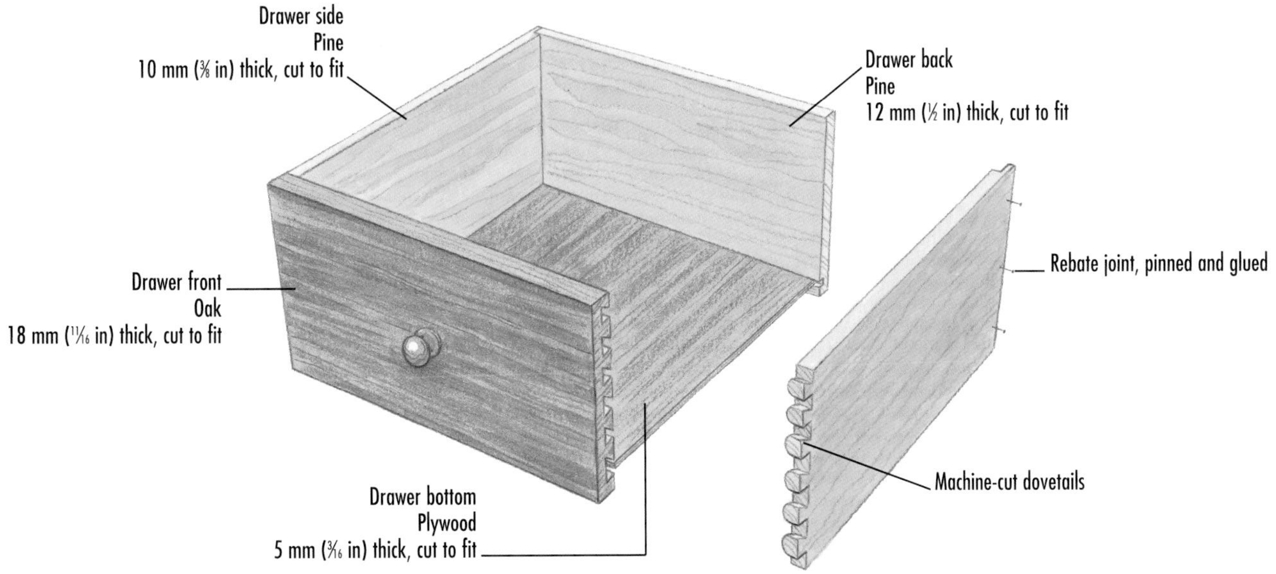
Drawer side
Pine
10 mm (⅜ in) thick, cut to fit
Drawer back
Pine
12 mm (½ in) thick, cut to fit
Rebate joint, pinned and glued
Drawer front
Oak
18 mm (11/16 in) thick, cut to fit
Machine-cut dovetails
Drawer bottom
Plywood
5 mm (3/16 in) thick, cut to fit

HOW TO MAKE THE BEDSIDE TABLE

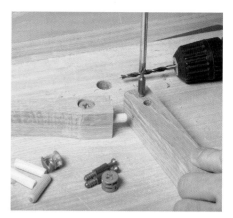

1 Preparing the wood

Cut and plane all the components for the carcass to the finished size. Use iron-on veneer edging strips to cover the exposed edges of the MDF used to make the tabletop of the cabinet (see page 117, step 7). Cut the curved shapes of the top and bottom rails on the bandsaw and shave them smooth with the spokeshave. Prepare the drawer components, but leave all the pieces over-length until after the joints have been cut.

2 Jointing the carcass

Use cam-dowel fixings to join the carcass components together. The dowels stop the rails from pivoting and add to the strength of the joints. Practise on offcuts to find the best position for the cam (the large, cylinder-shaped part of the fixing). Where possible, use a pillar drill to drill the holes, as this will achieve far more accurate results.

3 Assembling the carcass

Assemble the carcass, tighten the cam-dowel fixings and inspect the structure. Use a tape measure and try square to check for squareness. If all is fine, use the tape measure to check the size of the drawer openings. When calculating the drawer sizes, allow for a clearance gap of 1 mm (1/32 in) all around the front of the drawer.

4 Making and fitting the drawer runners

The drawer runners are two pieces of pine. They support the bottom of the drawer and guide the sides of the drawer. Use countersunk screws to fix them in position. Leave the carcass as it is until you have completed the drawers.

5 Cutting the dovetails on the router

We have used a dovetail jig to make the joints at the front of the drawers. Dovetail jigs do vary, but using them usually involves placing the front and side pieces together and routing them simultaneously, as shown above. The dovetail cutter has a bearing on the shaft that traces the finger shapes of the jig. Always practise on offcuts first, as the router setting is critical.

6 Cutting the rebates

Assemble the dovetail joints (without glue) and calculate how long the sides need to be in order to make a drawer of the correct length. Cut the sides to the finished length and make the rebate joints with the 10 mm (⅜ in) straight cutter and router table. Reassemble the drawers and calculate the finished length for the back pieces. Cut them to size.

7 Grooving the drawer

Use the router table and 5 mm (³⁄₁₆ in) straight cutter to make grooves in the bottoms of the drawer components. These grooves can run straight through the boards (they do not need to stop before the ends). Calculate the size of the drawer bottoms and cut out bottoms that are a slightly loose fit.

8 Gluing the drawer together

Set up the sash clamps so you are ready to glue up. Apply glue to the surfaces of the joints sparingly, assemble the dovetail joints, and slide the base into position followed by the back. Glue, clamp and check for squareness. Once dry, plane the joints level and check that they fit in the carcass. Take the carcass apart, sand and apply an oil finish to the components and the drawer fronts. Reassemble the carcass.

CHEST OF DRAWERS

Simple, classic designs are often the best option if you want a style that will not date. This American oak chest of drawers is constructed from a mixture of solid wood and pre-veneered MDF board (supplied with the veneer already stuck to both surfaces). A knock-down construction makes it easy to move.

YOU WILL NEED

- Table saw, planer and thicknesser (or buy prepared wood)
- Sliding compound mitre saw
- Bandsaw
- Spokeshave
- Router, router table, dovetail jig with cutter, 10 mm (⅜ in) and 5 mm (³⁄₁₆ in) straight cutters and a 10 mm (⅜ in) straight cutter with a guide bearing at the tip
- Pillar drill
- Crosshead screwdrivers
- Cordless driver, screwdriver bit, twist bits to suit cam-dowel fixings and dowels, and countersink bit
- Orbital sander, 80-grit and 600-grit sandpaper, sanding block
- Block plane
- Pencil, ruler, tape measure and try square
- Two sash clamps
- Rubber mallet
- Iron
- Wood: see drawing – oak, oak pre-veneered MDF, oak iron-on veneer edging strip, 8 oak knobs, pine
- Plastic joining blocks with screws: 4
- Cam-dowel fixings: 20
- Fluted dowels: 8 x 8 mm (⁵⁄₁₆ in)
- Screws: No. 8 cross-headed, zinc-plated, countersink: 8 x 20 mm (¹³⁄₁₆ in)
- PVA glue, water and cloth
- Finishing oil

GENERAL VIEW

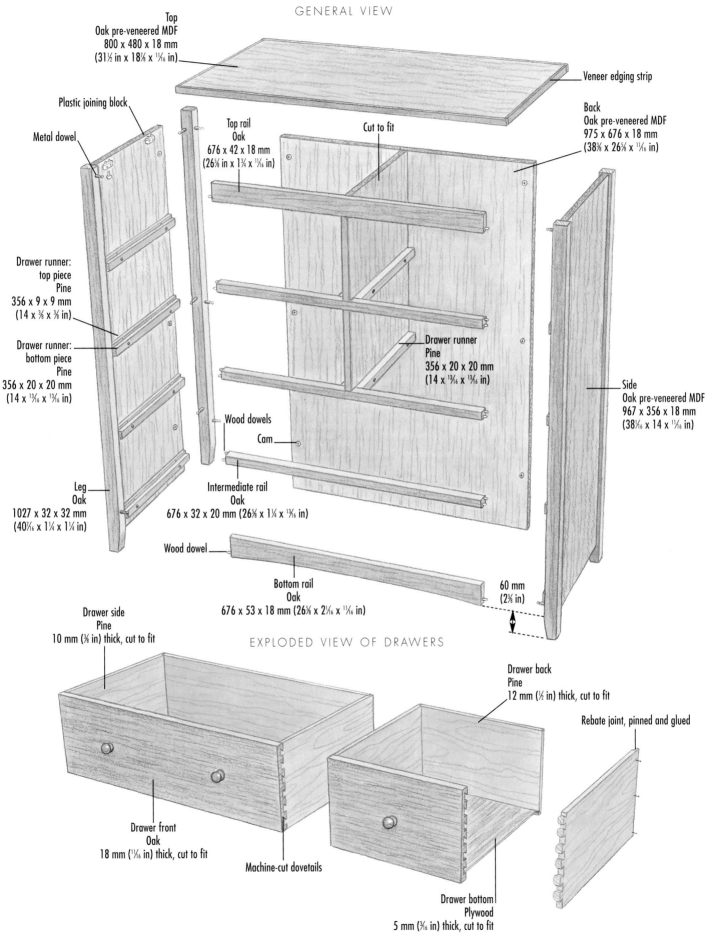

Top
Oak pre-veneered MDF
800 x 480 x 18 mm
(31½ in x 18⅞ x ¹¹⁄₁₆ in)

Veneer edging strip

Plastic joining block

Metal dowel

Top rail
Oak
676 x 42 x 18 mm
(26⅝ in x 1¾ x ¹¹⁄₁₆ in)

Cut to fit

Back
Oak pre-veneered MDF
975 x 676 x 18 mm
(38⅜ x 26⅝ x ¹¹⁄₁₆ in)

Drawer runner:
top piece
Pine
356 x 9 x 9 mm
(14 x ⅜ x ⅜ in)

Drawer runner:
bottom piece
Pine
356 x 20 x 20 mm
(14 x ¹³⁄₁₆ x ¹³⁄₁₆ in)

Drawer runner
Pine
356 x 20 x 20 mm
(14 x ¹³⁄₁₆ x ¹³⁄₁₆ in)

Side
Oak pre-veneered MDF
967 x 356 x 18 mm
(38¹⁄₁₆ x 14 x ¹¹⁄₁₆ in)

Wood dowels

Cam

Leg
Oak
1027 x 32 x 32 mm
(40⁷⁄₁₆ x 1¼ x 1¼ in)

Intermediate rail
Oak
676 x 32 x 20 mm (26⅝ x 1¼ x ¹³⁄₁₆ in)

Wood dowel

Bottom rail
Oak
676 x 53 x 18 mm (26⅝ x 2¹⁄₁₆ x ¹¹⁄₁₆ in)

60 mm
(2⅜ in)

Drawer side
Pine
10 mm (⅜ in) thick, cut to fit

EXPLODED VIEW OF DRAWERS

Drawer back
Pine
12 mm (½ in) thick, cut to fit

Rebate joint, pinned and glued

Drawer front
Oak
18 mm (¹¹⁄₁₆ in) thick, cut to fit

Machine-cut dovetails

Drawer bottom
Plywood
5 mm (³⁄₁₆ in) thick, cut to fit

HOW TO MAKE THE CHEST OF DRAWERS

1 Preparing the wood

Cut and plane all the components for the carcass to their finished size. When cutting the veneered board, experiment first to reduce break-out on the under-surface as the blade exits the wood. A backing board may help. Cut the tapers at the bottom of the legs on the bandsaw and use the block plane to flatten the surfaces.

2 Shaping the bottom rail

Cut the curved shape of the top rail on the bandsaw and shave it smooth with the spokeshave. Work inwards from each end so that you are working with the grain and not digging into it. Use sandpaper wrapped around a dowel or curved block to further smooth the surface.

3 Jointing the carcass

Use cam-dowel fixings to join the carcass components together. The dowels stop the rails from pivoting and add to the strength of the joints. Practise on offcuts to find the best position for the cam (the large, cylinder-shaped part of the fixing). If you do not have a pillar drill, place a try square beside the work as a guide for when you are drilling.

4 Assembling the carcass

Assemble the carcass, tighten the cam-dowel fixings and inspect the structure. Use a tape measure and try square to check for squareness. Fix the drawer runners as shown on page 112, step 4.

6 Making the drawers
Make the drawers using the dovetail jig and router table as explained on page 113.

5 Finishing the carcass
Disassemble the carcass. Use the block plane to plane off the sharp corners of the components (creating a bevelled edge). Sand all the outward-facing surfaces with the orbital sander. Finish with oil and reassemble. Use the tape measure to check the size of the drawer openings. When calculating the drawer sizes, allow for a clearance gap of 1 mm (1⁄32 in) all around the front of the drawer.

8 Trimming the veneer edge
Use the router and straight cutter with the bearing tip to trim the excess veneer flush with the surfaces. Use sandpaper and a sanding block to smooth over the sharp edges and corners. Sand the top with the orbital sander. Apply finishing oil to the top and the drawer fronts.

7 Edging the top
Use iron-on veneer edging to cover the exposed edges of the MDF used for the top of the chest of drawers. Press it down hard and work gradually from one end to the other. Follow up by using a block of wood to burnish the edge and ensure that the veneer stays firmly attached as the glue cools.

EMPIRE CHAIR

This traditional design will make an elegant addition to any sitting room or dining area. We have used oak, but you could opt for a dark wood such as walnut or cherry instead. This is the most challenging project in the book and will test even the most experienced chair-maker.

YOU WILL NEED

- Table saw, planer and thicknesser (or buy prepared wood)
- Mortiser and 10 mm (⅜ in) mortise chisel
- Sliding compound mitre saw
- Bandsaw
- Spokeshave
- Router, router table, and 10 mm (⅜ in) straight cutter (or use sliding compound mitre saw for cutting the tenons)
- Crosshead screwdrivers
- Chisel: 25 mm (1 in)
- Cordless driver, screwdriver bit, combination bit (drills counterbored clearance hole and pilot hole) and plug-cutter set to suit No. 8 screws and screwdriver bit
- Orbital sander, 80-grit and 600-grit sandpaper
- Smoothing plane and block plane
- Pencil, ruler, tape measure and try square
- Four sash clamps
- Rubber mallet
- Wood: see drawing – oak and plywood
- Screws: No. 8 cross-headed, zinc-plated, countersink: 10 x 40 mm (1⅟₆ in)
- Fluted dowels: 4 x 8 mm (⁵⁄₁₆ in)
- PVA glue, water and cloth
- Finishing oil and wax
- Oiling and polishing cloths

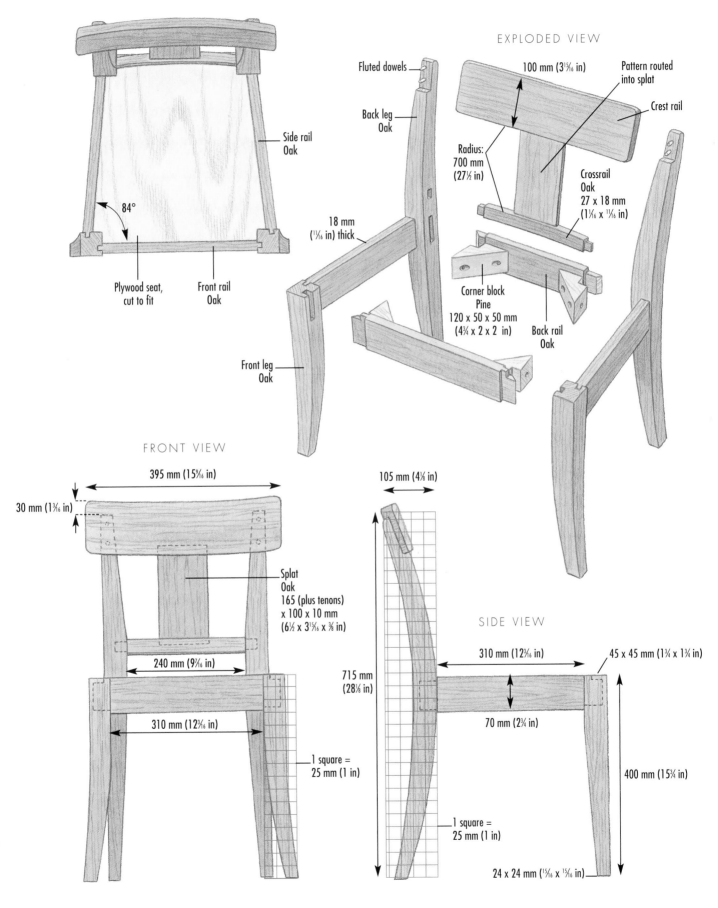

PLAN VIEW

Side rail
Oak

84°

Plywood seat,
cut to fit

Front rail
Oak

EXPLODED VIEW

Fluted dowels

Back leg
Oak

18 mm
(¹¹⁄₁₆ in) thick

Front leg
Oak

100 mm (3¹⁵⁄₁₆ in)

Pattern routed
into splat

Crest rail

Radius:
700 mm
(27½ in)

Crossrail
Oak
27 x 18 mm
(1¹⁄₁₆ x ¹¹⁄₁₆ in)

Corner block
Pine
120 x 50 x 50 mm
(4¾ x 2 x 2 in)

Back rail
Oak

FRONT VIEW

395 mm (15⁹⁄₁₆ in)

30 mm (1³⁄₁₆ in)

Splat
Oak
165 (plus tenons)
x 100 x 10 mm
(6½ x 3¹⁵⁄₁₆ x ⅜ in)

240 mm (9⁷⁄₁₆ in)

310 mm (12³⁄₁₆ in)

1 square =
25 mm (1 in)

105 mm (4⅛ in)

SIDE VIEW

715 mm
(28⅛ in)

310 mm (12³⁄₁₆ in)

45 x 45 mm (1¾ x 1¾ in)

70 mm (2¾ in)

400 mm (15¾ in)

1 square =
25 mm (1 in)

24 x 24 mm (¹⁵⁄₁₆ x ¹⁵⁄₁₆ in)

HOW TO MAKE THE EMPIRE CHAIR

1 Plotting the curved shapes

The legs are curved in one direction and tapered in another: the front legs are curved in the front view and tapered in the side view, and the back legs are curved in the side view and tapered in the front view. The tapering is easy to mark using the dimensions provided, but the curves are more difficult. Use the grids on the drawings as a guide. Draw a full-size grid on paper and plot the curves as shown.

2 Tracing the curved shapes

When you have finished plotting the curves on paper, cut out the pieces (improving the shape where possible) and use the shapes as templates to draw around on the wood. Flip them over to get the mirror image of the shape. The crest rail and crossrail can be drawn by using a home-made trammel (see page 59) to mark out the radius curves indicated in the drawing.

3 Mortising

Mark out the mortises on the legs, crest rail and crossrail. The mortises are cut with the mortiser before the components are cut into curved shapes. If you do forget to cut the joints first, you will have to work out a way of holding them firmly and squarely in the mortiser.

4 Cutting the curved and tapered shapes

Cut out the legs and back rails on the bandsaw. Work slowly and carefully, guiding the workpiece into the blade so that it cuts fractionally to the waste side of the pencil lines. It is better to plane off bumps than to have to reshape the whole piece by trying to iron out dips.

5 Planing and shaving the components

Use the smoothing plane and block plane to flatten and smooth the straight areas of the legs, and the spokeshave to smooth the curved areas. Oak is hard, so blades must be sharp for you to work efficiently. Check the smoothness of the curves by eye and by running your hand up and down the surface.

6 Cutting the tenon joints

Mark out the tenon joints on the seat rails and crossrail. Cut these out by hand or use the compound mitre saw or router table. Some of the tenons are angled, so check your markings carefully and practise first on scrap pieces of wood of the same section. Clean up the joints with the chisel and check that each fits accurately. Sand all components smooth.

7 Assembling

Practise assembling the chair and check that the joints close up completely and the structure is square. Make adjustments as necessary. We recommend that you glue the chair together in two stages: firstly, join the front legs to the front rail, and the back legs to the back rail and crossrail; and secondly join those two frames together using the side rails as shown above. Use sash clamps.

8 Completing the chair

Screw the crest rail to the top of the back legs and fill the screwholes with plugs of oak. When the glue has dried, shave and sand the plugs flush. Cut and fit the blocks inside the corners of the seat frame. These reinforce the structure and provide support for the plywood seat. Finish with two coats of oil and wax polish. Make a cushion to fit the shape of the seat.

CORNER DISPLAY CABINET

This is another simple, modern design made from solid maple and maple pre-veneered MDF. The single-panel door gives an unobstructed view of the cabinet's contents, and the combination of low-voltage lighting and glass shelves means that the cabinet is excellent for displaying ornaments.

YOU WILL NEED

- Table saw, planer and thicknesser (or buy prepared wood)
- Workbench with vice
- Sliding compound mitre saw
- Bandsaw
- Router, router table, and 10 mm (⅜ in) straight cutter
- Mortiser and 10 mm (⅜ in) mortise chisel
- Crosshead screwdrivers
- Cordless driver, screwdriver bit, and twist bits to suit shelf pegs and fixings
- Orbital sander, 80-grit and 600-grit sandpaper
- Smoothing plane and block plane
- Chisel
- Biscuit jointer and biscuits
- Pencil, ruler, tape measure, try square
- 8 sash clamps
- Wood: see drawing – maple, pine, maple pre-veneered MDF, maple iron-on veneer edging strip, pine
- Pins: 14 x 15 mm (1⁹⁄₁₆ in)
- Butt hinges: 2, with screws
- Knob and catch
- Shelf pegs to suit your requirements
- Plugs and screws for fixing to wall
- Glass: 820 x 540 x 4 mm (32⁵⁄₁₆ x 21¼ x ³⁄₁₆ in) for door; shelf glass is 6 mm (¼ in) thick, cut to fit (make template from offcut and take to glass supplier
- Fluorescent strip light kit, 200 mm (7⅞ in) long (suitable for a display cabinet; no electrical wiring work required)
- PVA glue, water and cloth
- Finishing oil and wax
- Oiling and polishing cloths

EXPLODED VIEW

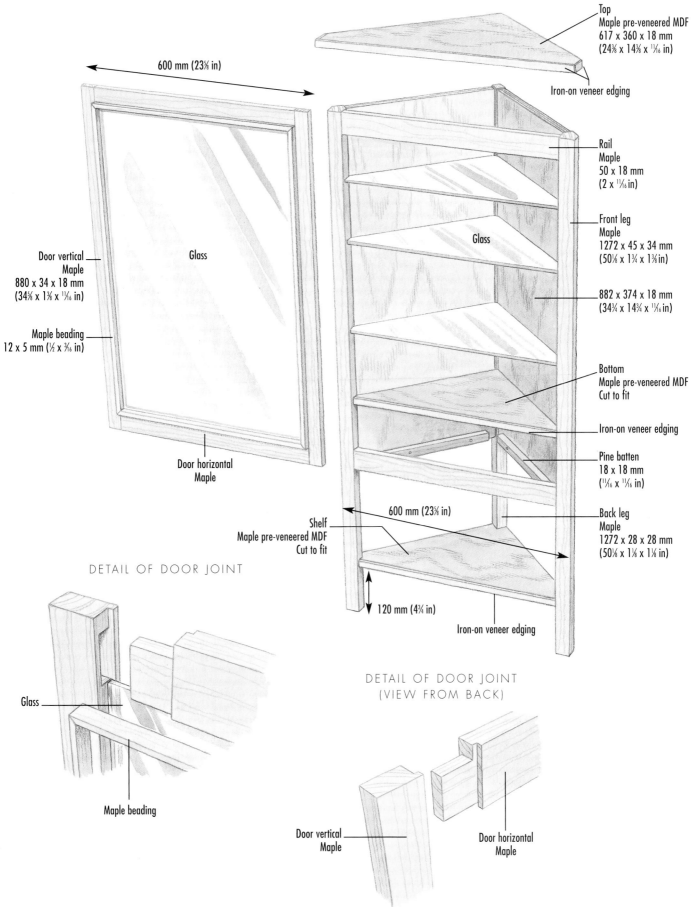

Top
Maple pre-veneered MDF
617 x 360 x 18 mm
(24⅜ x 14⅜ x ¹¹⁄₁₆ in)

Iron-on veneer edging

600 mm (23⅝ in)

Rail
Maple
50 x 18 mm
(2 x ¹¹⁄₁₆ in)

Front leg
Maple
1272 x 45 x 34 mm
(50⅛ x 1¾ x 1⅜ in)

Glass

882 x 374 x 18 mm
(34¾ x 14¾ x ¹¹⁄₁₆ in)

Door vertical
Maple
880 x 34 x 18 mm
(34⅝ x 1⅜ x ¹¹⁄₁₆ in)

Glass

Maple beading
12 x 5 mm (½ x ³⁄₁₆ in)

Bottom
Maple pre-veneered MDF
Cut to fit

Iron-on veneer edging

Pine batten
18 x 18 mm
(¹¹⁄₁₆ x ¹¹⁄₁₆ in)

Back leg
Maple
1272 x 28 x 28 mm
(50⅛ x 1⅛ x 1⅛ in)

Door horizontal
Maple

600 mm (23⅝ in)

Shelf
Maple pre-veneered MDF
Cut to fit

120 mm (4¾ in)

Iron-on veneer edging

DETAIL OF DOOR JOINT

Glass

Maple beading

DETAIL OF DOOR JOINT
(VIEW FROM BACK)

Door vertical
Maple

Door horizontal
Maple

123

HOW TO MAKE THE DISPLAY CABINET

1 Preparing the wood

Cut and plane the wood to size. Take care when cutting the pre-veneered MDF components to avoid damaging the edges. Mark the 45° angled faces on the ends of the front legs. Hold the legs in the vice while you plane off the waste wood (alternatively, you can achieve this shaping using a spindle moulder).

2 Cutting the joints

Mark and cut the mortises using the mortiser and 10 mm (⅜ in) mortise chisel. Practise cutting the corresponding tenons on the router table (or on the sliding compound mitre saw, or by hand). If necessary, use a chisel to trim the joint for a more accurate fit. Mark positions for adjustable shelf pegs on the sides of the cabinet (positions to suit your requirements) and drill the holes.

4 Cutting the housing joints

The shelf under the display cabinet is held in position using housing joints. These "slots" are cut using the sliding compound mitre saw. If possible, practise first on a scrap of wood of the same section to check your settings. Assemble the cabinet without glue and cut a bottom shelf to fit within the slots.

3 Biscuit jointing

The sides of the cabinet are joined to the legs using biscuit joints. Lay the legs alongside the cabinet sides, align them and mark the positions for the biscuits on both components at approximately 300 mm (11¹³⁄₁₆ in) intervals. Hold down the work with clamps and cut the slots with the biscuit jointer.

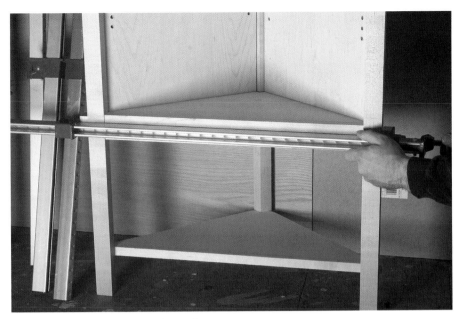

5 Gluing and assembling the carcass

Attach the battens to the sides of the cabinet. Cut a cabinet bottom and make sure it fits; cut notches at the corners to fit around the legs. Set up the sash clamps and practise clamping. When you are satisfied that the cabinet is ready to glue together, disassemble, sand smooth, apply glue to the joints and reasssemble. Clamp and check for squareness.

6 Making the door

Check the dimensions of the door by measuring the carcass. The door verticals can be left over-length and cut back once assembled (for a perfect finish). Use the router table to rebate the door sections. Mark the mortises and cut on the mortiser. Mark the tenons and cut on the sliding compound mitre saw. Clean out the corners of the mortises with the chisel.

7 Trimming the tenons

Use a chisel to shave off excess wood on the tenons. Check that each joint fits correctly; the shoulders of the tenons need to touch the sides of the verticals without leaving gaps that would reduce the strength of the joint.

8 Completing the cabinet

Assemble the door, check that it is flat and square and allow it to dry. Trim the end flush. Sand smooth, fit the glass and pin the beading in position. Hang the door. Give all surfaces another fine sanding, dust off and apply an oil and wax finish. Fit the light in the top of the cabinet. Use plugs and screws to fix the cabinet to the wall on each side.

125

GATELEG TABLE

Do you have a small living area with no room for a dining table? Maybe this folding gateleg table is the answer. Two stools can be stowed beneath the table (see page 130 for instructions on how to make the stool). When the flaps are raised, the size of the tabletop is more than doubled.

YOU WILL NEED

- Table saw, planer and thicknesser (or buy prepared wood)
- Sliding compound mitre saw
- Mortiser and 10 mm (⅜ in) mortise chisel
- Bandsaw
- Router table, router and 10 mm (⅜ in) straight cutter
- Cordless driver, screwdriver bit, and twist bits to suit screws
- Orbital sander, 80-grit and 600-grit sandpaper
- Biscuit jointer and biscuits
- Chisel
- Pencil, ruler, tape measure and try square
- Five sash clamps and a fast-clamp
- Wood: see drawing – pine, MDF
- Expansion plates: 6
- Penny washers: 8
- Screws to fit expansion plates, blocks and washers
- Butt hinges: 4
- Piano hinges: 2
- Swivelling castors: 6
- PVA glue, water and cloth
- Varnish

GENERAL VIEW

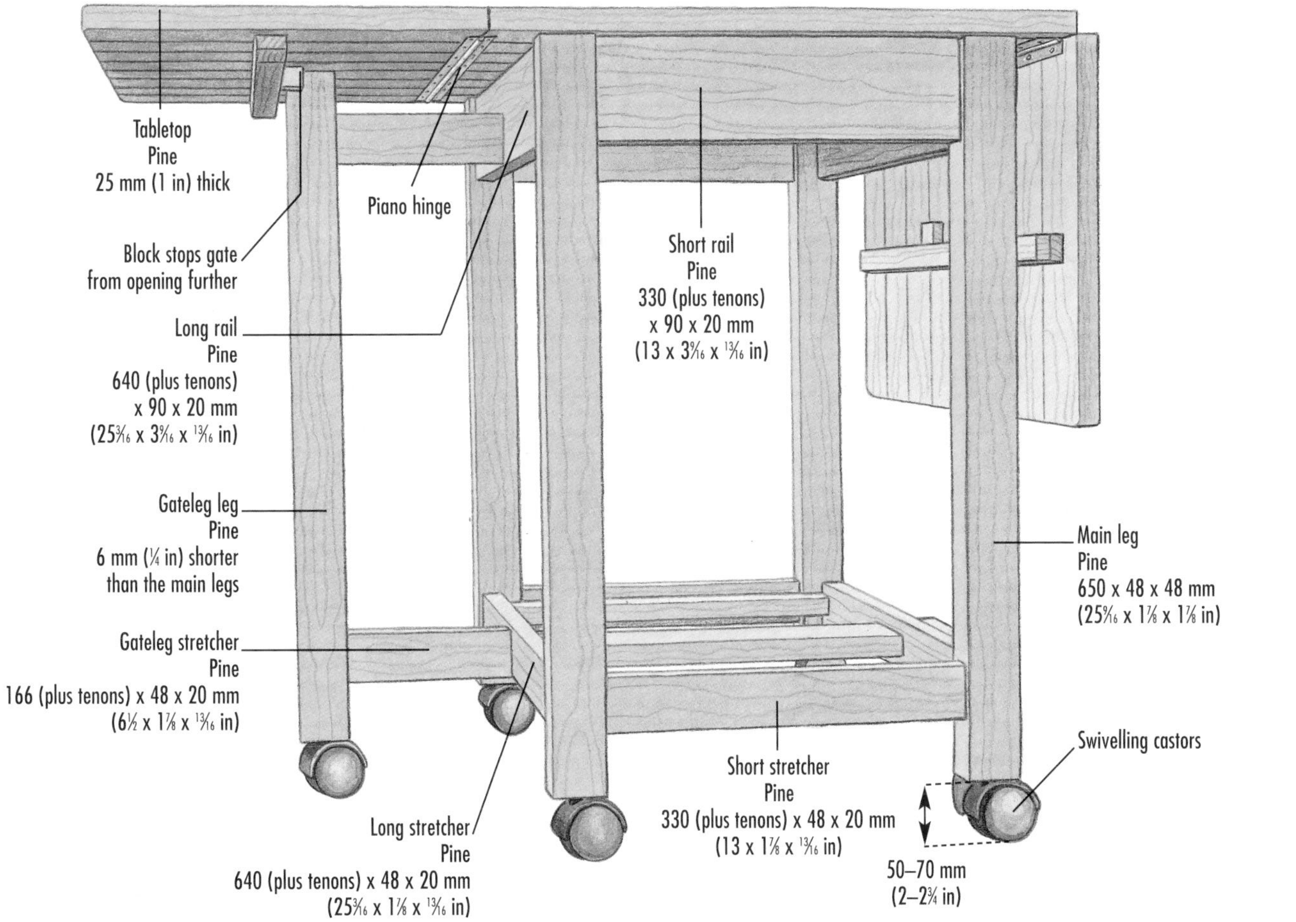
Tabletop
Pine
25 mm (1 in) thick
Piano hinge
Block stops gate from opening further
Long rail
Pine
640 (plus tenons) x 90 x 20 mm
(25 3/16 x 3 9/16 x 13/16 in)
Short rail
Pine
330 (plus tenons) x 90 x 20 mm
(13 x 3 9/16 x 13/16 in)
Gateleg leg
Pine
6 mm (1/4 in) shorter than the main legs
Main leg
Pine
650 x 48 x 48 mm
(25 9/16 x 1 7/8 x 1 7/8 in)
Gateleg stretcher
Pine
166 (plus tenons) x 48 x 20 mm
(6 1/2 x 1 7/8 x 13/16 in)
Swivelling castors
Short stretcher
Pine
330 (plus tenons) x 48 x 20 mm
(13 x 1 7/8 x 13/16 in)
Long stretcher
Pine
640 (plus tenons) x 48 x 20 mm
(25 3/16 x 1 7/8 x 13/16 in)
50–70 mm
(2–2 3/4 in)

PLAN VIEW

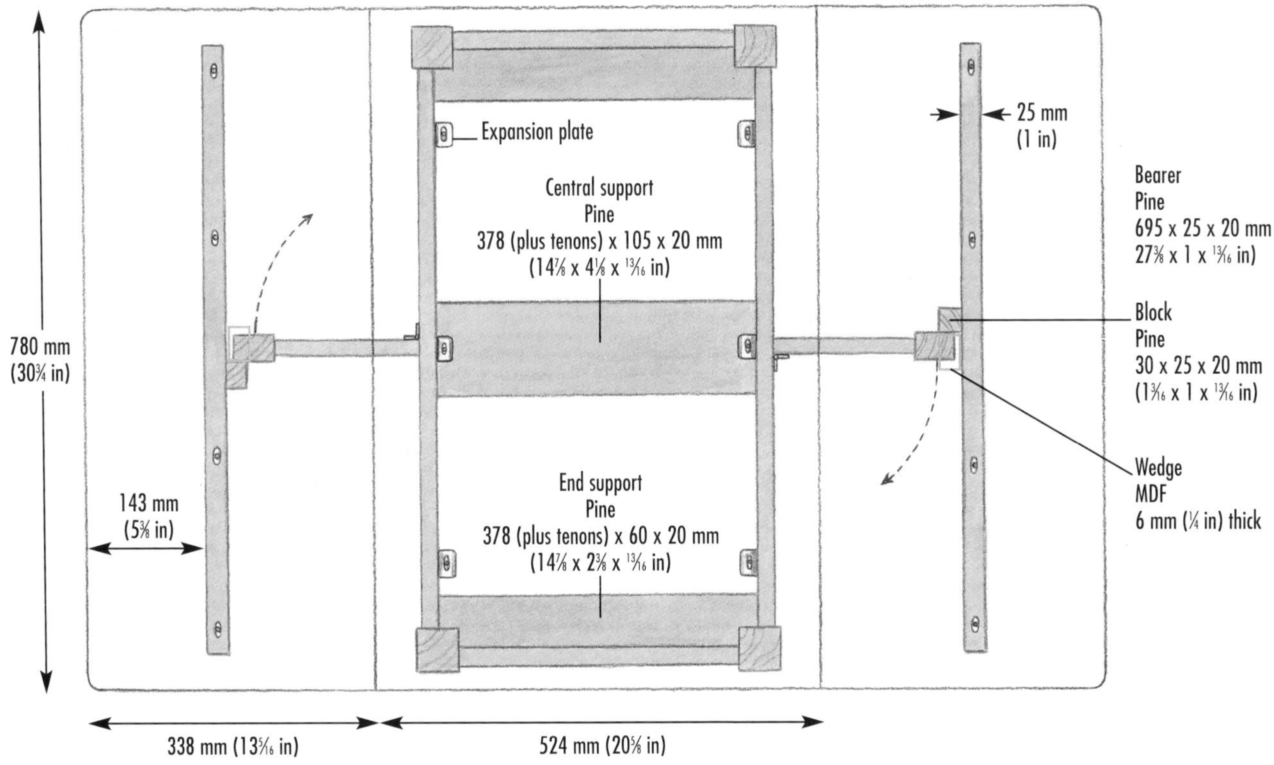
Expansion plate
Central support
Pine
378 (plus tenons) x 105 x 20 mm
(14 7/8 x 4 1/8 x 13/16 in)
End support
Pine
378 (plus tenons) x 60 x 20 mm
(14 7/8 x 2 3/8 x 13/16 in)
25 mm
(1 in)
Bearer
Pine
695 x 25 x 20 mm
27 3/8 x 1 x 13/16 in)
Block
Pine
30 x 25 x 20 mm
(1 3/16 x 1 x 13/16 in)
Wedge
MDF
6 mm (1/4 in) thick
780 mm
(30 3/4 in)
143 mm
(5 5/8 in)
338 mm (13 5/16 in)
524 mm (20 5/8 in)

HOW TO MAKE THE GATELEG TABLE

2 Mitring the tenons

Mitre the tenons on the ends of the table rails using the compound mitre saw set at 45°. When fitted, the ends of the mitred tenons must not touch inside the joint (there should be a gap of approximately 2 mm (1/16 in).

1 Cutting the mortise and tenon joints

Prepare the legs and rails for the table. Use the mortise chisel to mark out the mortises on the legs. Cut the mortises and clean them out with a chisel. Set the router table and straight cutter to produce tenons that fit accurately. Practise on a scrap piece and test the fit. When you are satisfied, cut all the tenons.

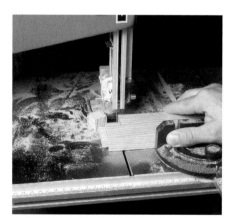

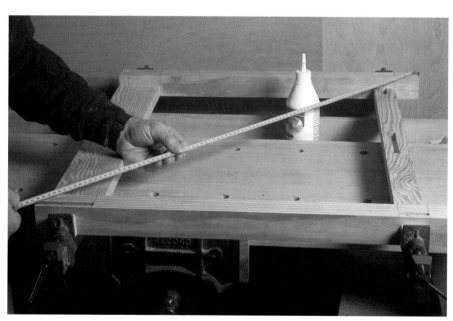

3 Notching the tenons

Use the bandsaw to cut notches in the ends of the tenons where required. The 90° guide on the bandsaw is useful for this; it is better to cut off fractionally less than you need and trim back later with a chisel. Check that the joints fit together correctly.

4 Assembling the table frame (first stage)

When you are satisfied that the table frame fits together correctly (practise assembling it without glue), prepare to glue the sides of the frame together as shown above (this is easier than attempting to glue the whole frame in one go). Spread glue in the mortises, apply the clamps and check for squareness with a tape measure.

5 Assembling the table frame (second stage)

When the two frame sides are dry, remove the clamps and practise assembling the complete frame as shown above. Apply glue to the mortises and tighten the clamps. Check that the frame is square: use the try square to check the inside corners and the tape measure to make sure that the diagonals are equal in length.

6 Gluing the top together

Prepare boards for the tabletop; keep them at least 25 mm (1 in) longer than the finished size. Arrange the boards so the direction of the end-grain growth rings alternates (one curves upwards, the next downwards etc.) and the grain pattern of adjacent boards blends. Label them in order and mark positions for biscuit joints. Cut the biscuit slots, practise clamping to check the joints, and then glue and clamp (see pages 70–72).

7 Attaching the gateleg frames

Glue together the gateleg frames and allow to dry. The legs of these frames should be 6 mm (¼ in) shorter than the other legs, leaving a 6 mm (¼ in) gap between the top of the leg and the underside of the surface. Attach the gateleg frames to the main table frame with butt hinges.

8 Completing the table

Cut the tabletop to size. Cut through the top to divide it into three pieces. Sand the surfaces and edges smooth. Sand the rest of the table. Screw the bearers, wedge and blocks to the underside of the flaps. Fix the table frame to the tabletop. Attach the flaps to the tabletop with piano hinges. Finish with several coats of varnish.

STOOL

This great little stool is strong, unlikely to tip over and very useful to have around the house – both for sitting and standing on. It is the same height as a normal chair and can be used with the table on page 126 (two fit under the table). We have used furniture-grade southern yellow pine, which has few knots.

YOU WILL NEED

- Table saw, planer and thicknesser (or buy prepared wood)
- Sliding compound mitre saw
- Mortiser and 10 mm (⅜ in) mortise chisel
- Bandsaw or tenon saw
- Pin hammer
- Chisel
- Pillar drill and 25 mm (1 in) forstner bit
- Router, router table, 10 mm (⅜ in) straight cutter and round-over cutter
- Cordless driver, screwdriver bit, 6 mm (¼ in) twist bit, and a combination bit (drills counterbored clearance hole and pilot hole) and plug-cutter set to suit No. 8 screws and screwdriver bit
- Orbital sander, 80-grit and 600-grit sandpaper
- Pencil, ruler, tape measure and try square
- Four sash clamps, two G-clamps and one fast-clamp
- Wood: see drawing – pine and pine dowelling 1220 x 25 mm (48 x 1 in)
- Screws: No. 8 cross-headed, zinc-plated, countersink: 4 x 50 mm (2 in)
- Pins: 2 x 30 mm (1³⁄₆ in)
- Dowel: 400 x 6 mm (15¾ x ¼ in) in diameter
- PVA glue, water and cloth
- Varnish

FRONT VIEW

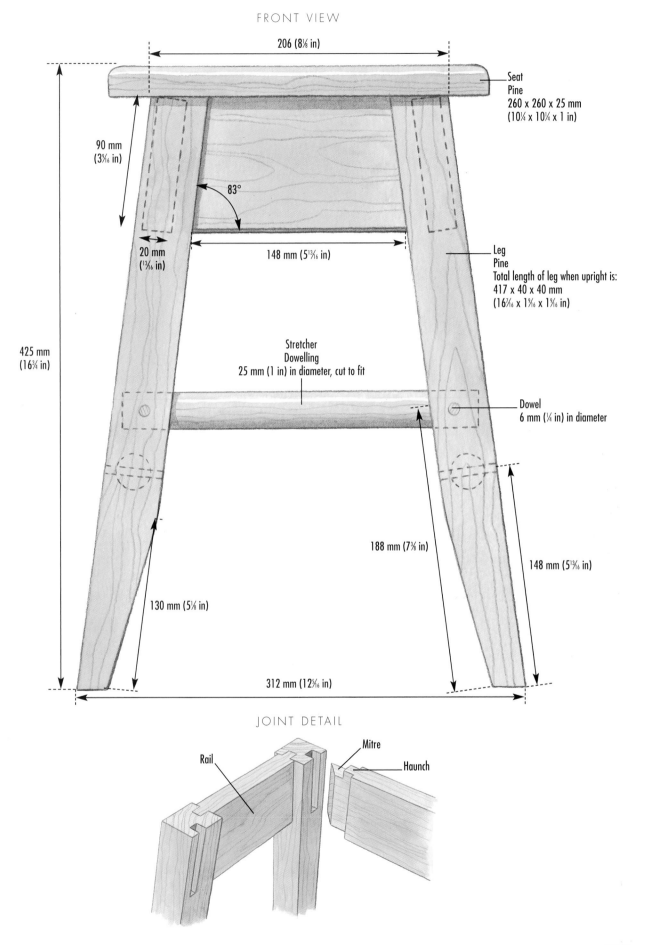

206 (8⅛ in)

Seat
Pine
260 x 260 x 25 mm
(10¼ x 10¼ x 1 in)

90 mm
(3⁹⁄₁₆ in)

83°

Leg
Pine
Total length of leg when upright is:
417 x 40 x 40 mm
(16⁷⁄₁₆ x 1⁹⁄₁₆ x 1⁹⁄₁₆ in)

20 mm
(¹³⁄₁₆ in)

148 mm (5¹³⁄₁₆ in)

Stretcher
Dowelling
25 mm (1 in) in diameter, cut to fit

425 mm
(16¾ in)

Dowel
6 mm (¼ in) in diameter

188 mm (7⅜ in)

148 mm (5¹³⁄₁₆ in)

130 mm (5⅛ in)

312 mm (12⁵⁄₁₆ in)

JOINT DETAIL

Rail

Mitre

Haunch

HOW TO MAKE THE STOOL

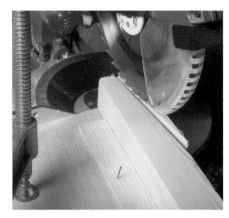

1 Tapering the legs

Prepare the legs and rails, leaving them all slightly over-length – 10 mm (⅜ in) or more. Make a simple jig for cutting the tapers on the legs on the compound mitre saw: the baseboard and strip can be made from offcuts. Use G-clamps to hold the workpiece, and keep your hands well away from the blade. After cutting the first taper, turn the leg through 90° and cut the second taper.

2 Mortising the legs

Mark out the positions of the mortises in the legs with the tape measure, try square and pencil. Make the first plunge at one end of the mortise; several plunges are needed to clear out the wood to the required depth. Reposition the wood and make the second series of plunges at the other end of the mortise. Mortise out the area remaining. Complete the mortises on all four legs.

3 Cutting the rails

Set up the compound mitre saw to cut the angled ends on the rails, which form the ends of the tenons. Cut the angle on one end of all the rails before resetting the saw for cutting the angles on the other ends. For greater accuracy, use an end-stop to ensure that all rails are precisely the same length.

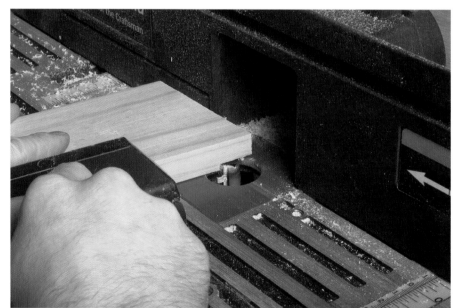

4 Routing the tenons

Mount the router in the router table and use the 10 mm (⅜ in) straight cutter to cut tenons on the ends of the rails. The guide must be set at the correct angle to present the end of the rail so it is parallel with the fence of the router table.

5 Drilling the holes in the legs

Use the tape measure and pencil to mark the centre points of the holes in the legs. Make an angled jig from scraps of wood, as shown above, to support the legs at the correct angle.

6 Trimming the tops of the legs

Set the compound mitre saw to cut the compound angle at the top of the legs (head tilted and table rotated). Cut each leg to the finished length, top and bottom.

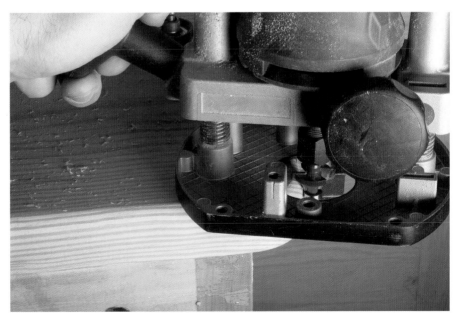

7 Assembling

It is best to assemble the stool in two stages: first, glue both side frames and allow to dry, then join them together using the remaining parts, as shown above. (Set up the clamps to the correct distance and practise clamping without glue before you proceed.) When the glue has dried, remove the clamps and use dowels to reinforce the joints of the dowelling stretchers (see drawing).

8 Finishing

Use the router and the round-over cutter to create rounded edges on the top of the seat. Attach the seat, driving four screws through the top and into the rails. Conceal the heads of the screws with solid pine plugs; make these from offcuts, using the plug-cutter in the pillar drill. Sand everything smooth and apply several coats of varnish to the stool.

GARDEN BENCH

This is nothing like those cheap, fragile benches made from tropical hardwood that you see so often. This one is generously proportioned, solid as a rock and made entirely from American oak. The design on the back rail is achieved using a special "carving" router cutter and template kit.

YOU WILL NEED

- Table saw, planer and thicknesser (or buy prepared wood)
- Sliding compound mitre saw
- Mortiser and 10 mm (⅜ in) mortise chisel
- Bandsaw or tenon saw
- Router, router table, 10 mm (⅜ in) straight cutter, round-over cutter, "carving" cutter and templates (or carving gouges)
- Cordless driver, screwdriver bit, and a combination bit (drills a counterbored clearance hole and pilot hole) and plug-cutter set to suit No. 8 screws and screwdriver bit
- Orbital sander, 80-grit and 600-grit sandpaper
- Smoothing plane and block plane
- Spokeshave
- Chisels
- Pencil, ruler, tape measure and try square
- Eight sash clamps and one fast-clamp
- Wood: see drawing – oak
- Screws: No.8 cross-headed, stainless-steel, countersink: 48 x 38 mm (1½ in)
- PVA glue, water and cloth
- Preservative finish

FRONT VIEW OF TOP RAIL

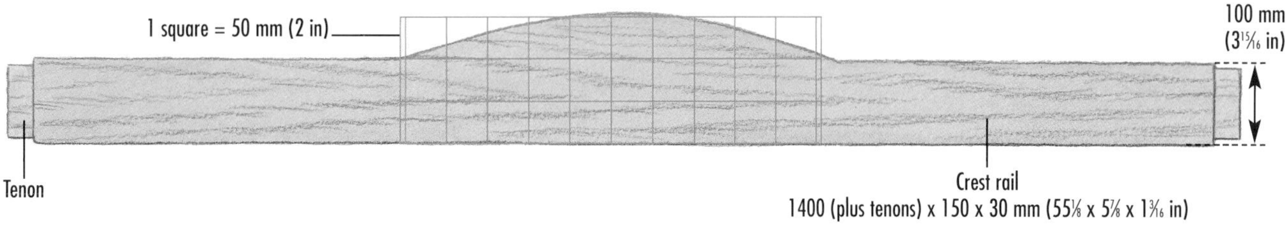
1 square = 50 mm (2 in)
100 mm (3 15/16 in)
Tenon
Crest rail
1400 (plus tenons) x 150 x 30 mm (55 1/8 x 5 7/8 x 1 3/16 in)

FRONT VIEW

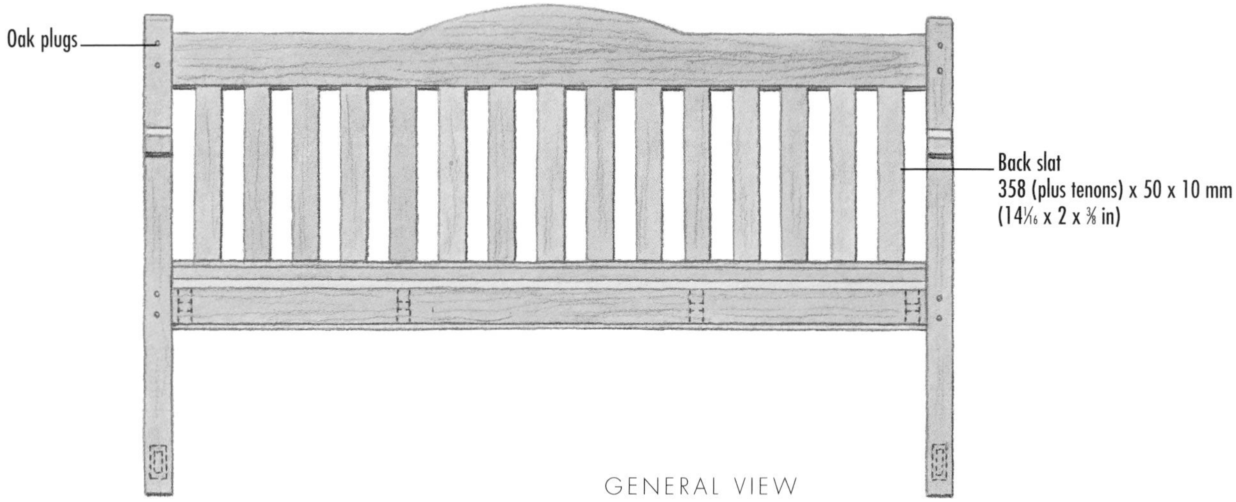
Oak plugs
Back slat
358 (plus tenons) x 50 x 10 mm
(14 1/16 x 2 x 3/8 in)

GENERAL VIEW

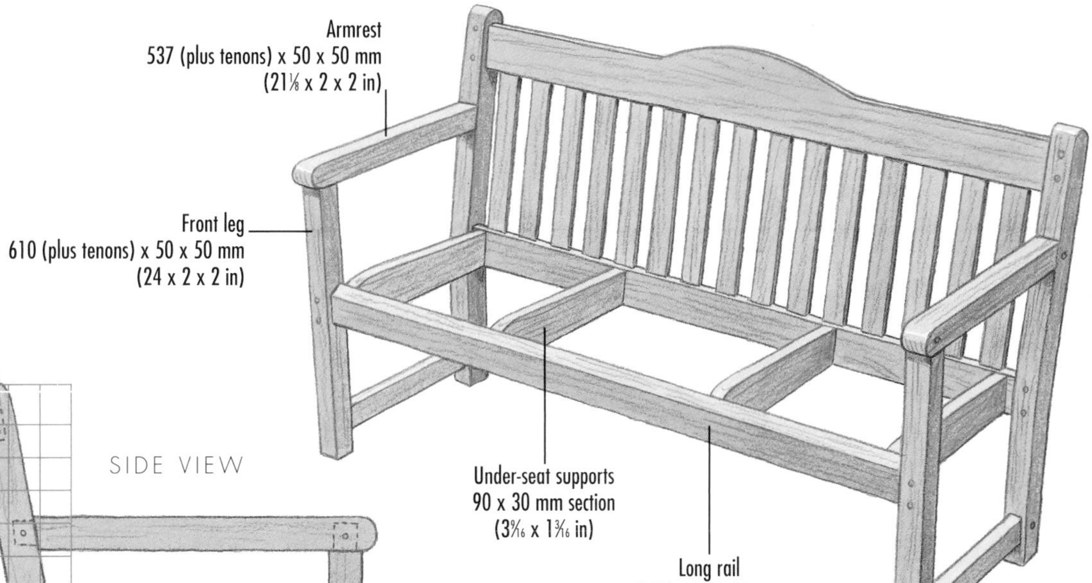
Armrest
537 (plus tenons) x 50 x 50 mm
(21 1/8 x 2 x 2 in)
Front leg
610 (plus tenons) x 50 x 50 mm
(24 x 2 x 2 in)
Under-seat supports
90 x 30 mm section
(3 9/16 x 1 3/16 in)
Long rail
1400 x 80 x 30 mm
(55 1/8 x 3 1/8 x 1 3/16 in)

SIDE VIEW

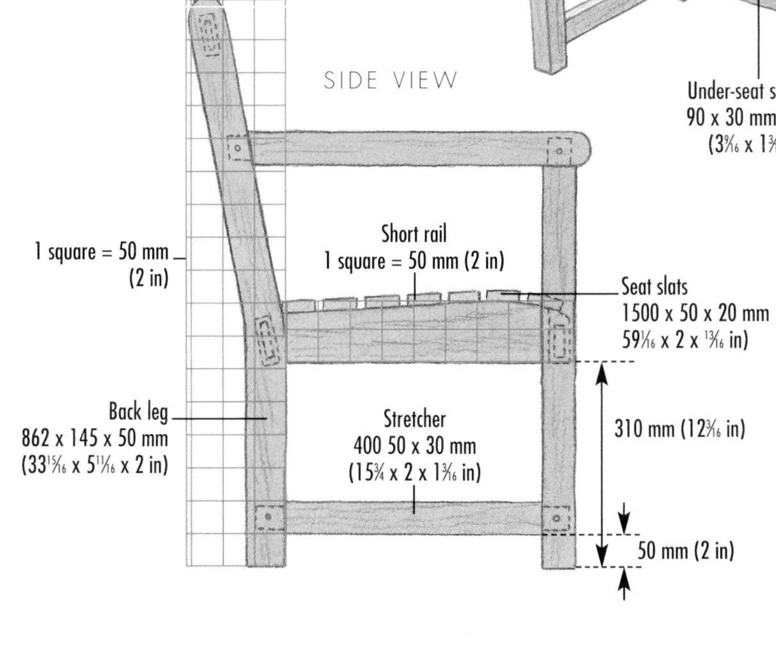
1 square = 50 mm
(2 in)
Short rail
1 square = 50 mm (2 in)
Seat slats
1500 x 50 x 20 mm
59 1/16 x 2 x 13/16 in)
Back leg
862 x 145 x 50 mm
(33 15/16 x 5 11/16 x 2 in)
Stretcher
400 50 x 30 mm
(15 3/4 x 2 x 1 3/16 in)
310 mm (12 3/16 in)
50 mm (2 in)

HOW TO MAKE THE GARDEN BENCH

1 Preparing the wood

Cut and plane the components to size. Mark out the shape of the back legs, cut them out with the bandsaw and plane smooth with the smoothing plane and the block plane.

2 Cutting the mortises in the top rail

Before cutting the curved shape on the crest rail, first cut the mortise joints. Mark out the positions of the 10 mm (⅜ in) mortises and cut them out with the mortiser. Use chisels to clean out the remaining waste from either end of the mortises to leave a clean, rectangular hole.

3 Shaping the crest rail

Mark out the shape of the crest rail, using the grid on the drawing as a guide. Cut the curved shape on the bandsaw, working close to the drawn line but not going over it. Plane back to a smooth finish with the spokeshave.

4 Other mortises

Mark out the positions of the other mortises on the bench components. Cut these out on the mortiser. Mark out the position of the corresponding tenons.

5 Tenoning the components

Use the router, router table and 10 mm (⅜ in) straight cutter to cut the tenons on the bench components. Before actually cutting a tenon, practise first on a scrap of wood of the same thickness to check that your set-up produces a tightly fitting joint. Adjust the router table as necessary.

6 Cutting the support tenons

The tenons on the under-seat supports can be cut on the bandsaw rather than on the router table. The fence and 90° guide will help you to cut these joints, but take great care to avoid cutting away too much material. If in doubt, practise on a scrap piece of oak first and check the fit in the corresponding mortise.

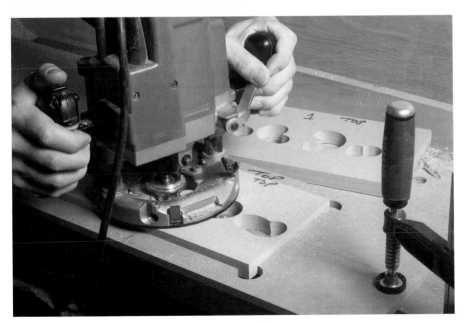

7 Routing the pattern in the crest rail

The decoration in the centre of the crest rail is created using a special "carving" cutter and template in the router (see list of suppliers on page 175). Choose a pattern and follow the instructions provided. Alternatively, carve your own pattern with carving gouges (see woodcarving techniques, page 88).

8 Assembling and finishing

Use the router and round-over cutter to produce rounded edges on the seat slats. Sand all components smooth. Practise assembling and clamping the frame without glue. Glue, clamp, check the frame is square, and allow to dry. Screw the seat slats in position. Apply a finish suited to outdoor furniture. We recommend using a preservative finish that seals the wood, rather than just oil.

LAMINATED TROLLEY

Put an end to juggling with cups, glasses and plates and make yourself this 1930s-style laminated beech and birch trolley instead. This apparently simple design is a challenging woodworking project; making the formers for laminating the frame requires a great deal of accuracy.

YOU WILL NEED

- Table saw, planer and thicknesser (or buy prepared wood)
- Sliding compound mitre saw
- Bandsaw
- Jigsaw
- Router and 10 mm (⅜ in) straight cutter with a guide bearing at the tip
- Crosshead screwdriver
- Cordless driver, screwdriver bit, and combination bit (drills a counterbored clearance hole and pilot hole) and plug-cutter set to suit No. 8 screws and screwdriver bit
- Orbital sander, 80-grit and 600-grit sandpaper
- Smoothing plane and block plane
- Chisel
- Pencil, ruler, tape measure and try square
- Eight G-clamps
- Wood: see drawing – beech and birch constructional veneer; plywood for former
- Screws: No. 8 cross-headed, zinc-plated, countersink: 70 x 38 mm (1½ in) for making formers; 16 x 38 mm (1½ in)
- Castors: 4
- PVA glue, water and cloth
- Varnish and wax
- Brushes and polishing cloths

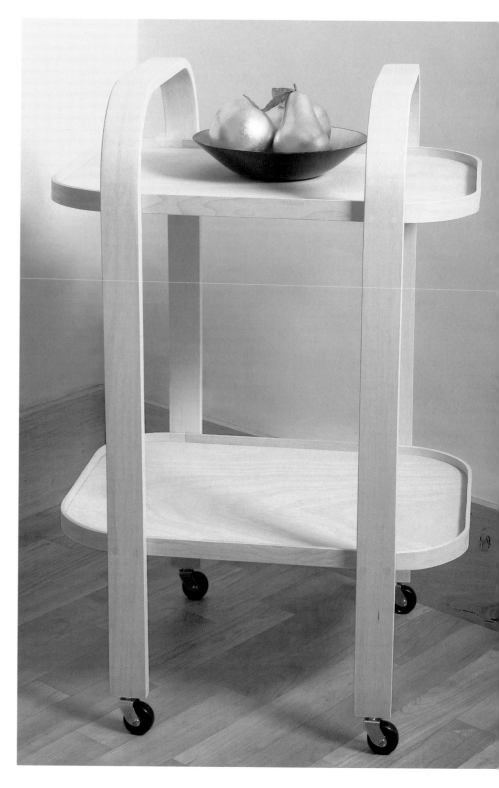

GENERAL VIEW

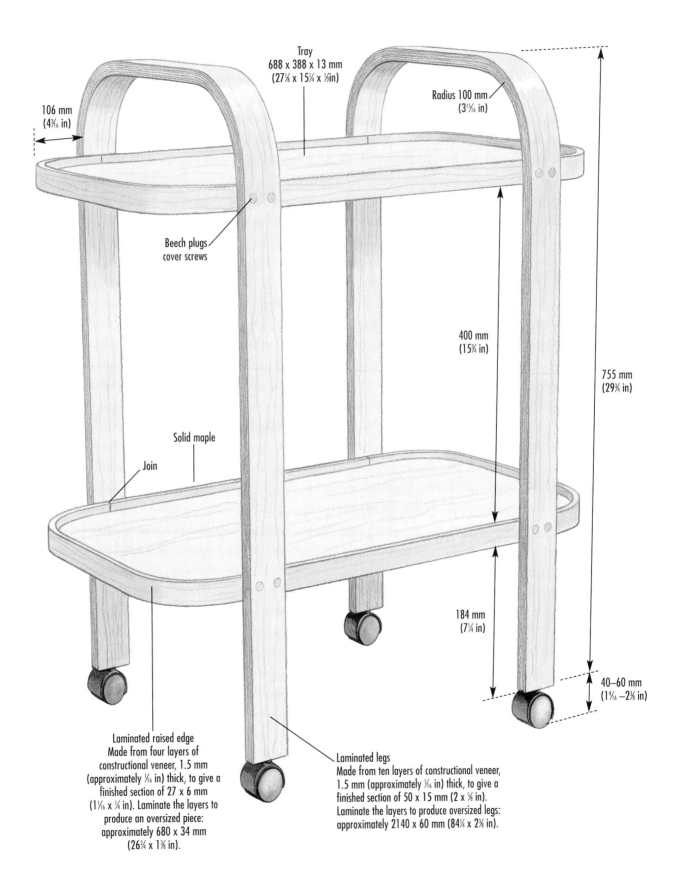

Tray
688 x 388 x 13 mm
(27⅛ x 15¼ x ½in)

Radius 100 mm
(3¹⁵⁄₁₆ in)

106 mm
(4³⁄₁₆ in)

Beech plugs
cover screws

400 mm
(15¾ in)

755 mm
(29¾ in)

Solid maple

Join

184 mm
(7¼ in)

40–60 mm
(1⁹⁄₁₆ –2⅜ in)

Laminated raised edge
Made from four layers of
constructional veneer, 1.5 mm
(approximately ¹⁄₁₆ in) thick, to give a
finished section of 27 x 6 mm
(1¹⁄₁₆ x ¼ in). Laminate the layers to
produce an oversized piece:
approximately 680 x 34 mm
(26¾ x 1⅜ in).

Laminated legs
Made from ten layers of constructional veneer,
1.5 mm (approximately ¹⁄₁₆ in) thick, to give a
finished section of 50 x 15 mm (2 x ⅝ in).
Laminate the layers to produce oversized legs:
approximately 2140 x 60 mm (84¼ x 2⅜ in).

HOW TO MAKE THE LAMINATED TROLLEY

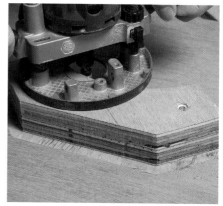

1 Making the leg former: 1
The laminated leg former is made out of multiple layers of identically shaped pieces of plywood. It measures 795 x 400 mm (31⁵⁄₁₆ x 15¾ in) with 100 mm (3¹⁵⁄₁₆ in) radii. Mark and cut the first layer of the centre block as accurately as you can. Reproduce this shape as follows: cut out a new shape roughly 2 mm (¹⁄₁₆ in) bigger all around, fix to a base (scrap) with screws, then place the original centrally and fix with screws. Use the router and bearing-tipped cutter to trace around the original.

2 Making the leg former: 2
Mark out the blocks that will shape the outer corners of the curved part of the legs. They measure 175 x 175 mm (6⅞ x 6⅞ in). Stack the ten layers of constructional veneer for the legs; check that the overall thickness is as prescribed. Increase the corner radius measurement of the block by this amount. Reproduce this shape (and its mirror image) as described for the centre block in step 1.

3 Assembling the leg former
Fix the layers of the central section to a baseboard (scrap) with glue and screws. Fix the corner blocks together with glue and screws. Allow the glue to dry. Drill holes (to accept the feet of the G-clamps) in the central section. Cut the straight blocks: top block is 200 x 60 x 60 mm (7⅞ x 2⅜ x 2⅜ in); side blocks are 695 x 60 x 60 mm (27⅜ x 2⅜ x 2⅜ in). Apply a varnish and wax polish finish to all parts of the former.

4 Laminating the legs
Cut the pieces of constructional veneer for the legs to the oversized sizes given on the drawing. Practise bending and clamping them. Mark centre-lines on the outer pieces of veneer to help you position the stack. When you are confident to go ahead, spread glue on the veneers, stack them up and position them in the former. Tighten the clamps on the central section first, then the corners, and finish with the straight sections.

5 Planing the legs

Use a smoothing plane, set for a coarse cut, to flatten and smooth one side of the legs. Continue planing until you have removed all uneven edges and traces of glue. Mark the finished width of the legs and start planing the other side. Continue until you have removed all the waste. Reset the plane for a fine cut and smooth both edges. Cut to length on the compound mitre saw.

6 Making the edges of the trays

The raised edges of the tray are laminated in the same way as the legs. The former is smaller but very similar. The central section is 388 x 120 mm (15¼ x 4¾ in) with 100 mm (3¹⁵⁄₁₆ in) radii. The two corner blocks are 161 x 141 mm (6⅜ x 5⁹⁄₁₆ in). The top block is 288 x 35 x 35 mm (11⁵⁄₁₆ x 1⅜ x 1⅜ in). Make in the same way as before. Laminate four layers of constructional veneer to make these components and plane them level as before. Leave them slightly wider than their finished size.

7 Edging the trays

Cut the laminated parts of the raised edging to length and attach to the tray with glue; clamp. When dry, remove the clamps. Cut straight pieces of solid wood, 27 x 6 mm (1¹⁄₁₆ x ¼ in) to fit between the laminated parts and complete the raised edging. Glue, clamp and allow to dry. Use the block plane to make the edging level all around and flush with the bottom of the tray.

8 Assembling

Mark the location of the trays on the legs. Drill counterbored holes for the screws, using a combination bit that drills a counterbored clearance hole which can be filled with a solid plug of wood, and also drills a pilot hole at the same time. Sand all the components. Assemble the trolley. Glue in the plugs to cover the screwheads, allow to dry and shave flush with a chisel. Fine-sand everything and apply a varnish finish.

WRITING DESK

The inspiration for this design came from Art Deco desks that used hollow construction and decorative veneers to give the impression of large, solid shapes. This desk has a cupboard either side for storing paperwork and housing a computer tower (CPU), and a central pull-out keyboard shelf.

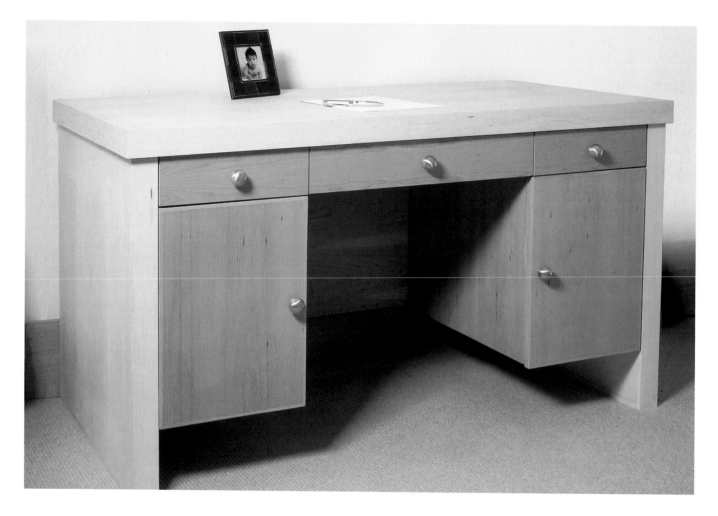

YOU WILL NEED

- Table saw, planer and thicknesser (or buy prepared wood)
- Sliding compound mitre saw
- Bandsaw
- Router table or spindle moulder
- Cabinet scraper
- Router and 15 mm (⅝ in), 10 mm (⅜ in) and 5 mm (³⁄₁₆ in) straight cutters
- Crosshead screwdriver
- Cordless driver, screwdriver bit, and twist bits to suit shelf pegs and fixings

- Orbital sander, 80-grit and 600-grit sandpaper, and sanding block
- Smoothing plane and block plane
- Dowels or dovetail jig for making drawers
- Chisel
- Biscuit jointer and biscuits
- Pencil, ruler, tape measure and try square
- Four sash clamps
- Wood: see drawing – cherry, pine, maple; maple and cherry pre-veneered MDF; plywood

- European-style concealed hinges, with screws: 4
- Drawer runners: 3 pairs
- Cam-dowel fixings: 6
- Backflap hinges: 2
- Screws: No. 8 cross-headed, zinc-plated, countersink: 12 x 40 mm (1⅝ in)
- Knobs and catches of your choice
- Shelf pegs to suit your requirements
- PVA glue, water and cloth
- Finishing oil and wax; cloths
- Fine wire wool

EXPLODED VIEW

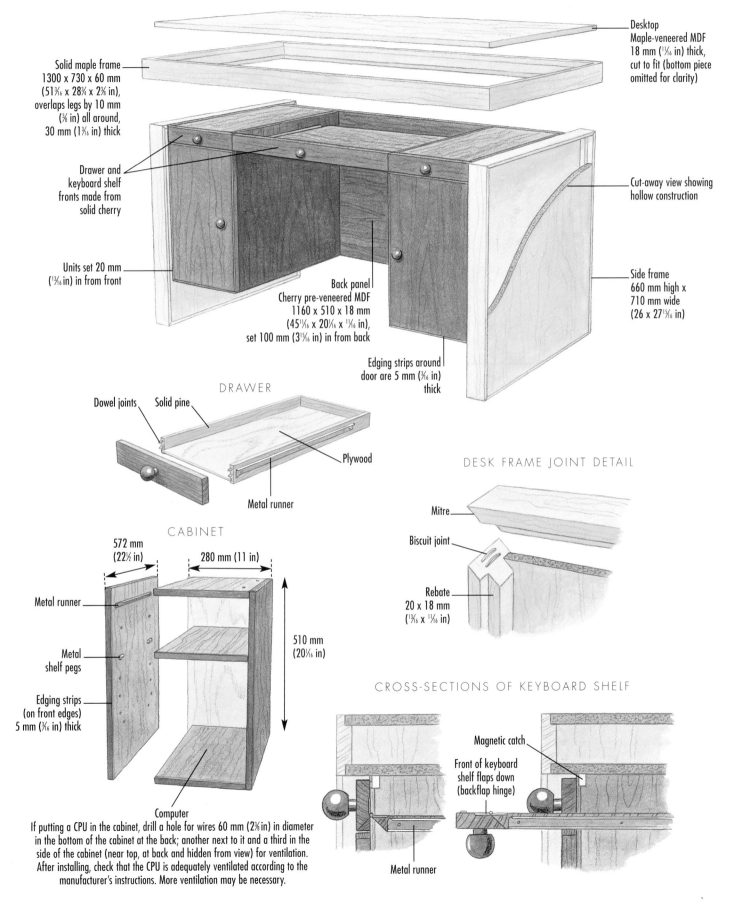

Desktop
Maple-veneered MDF
18 mm (¹¹⁄₁₆ in) thick,
cut to fit (bottom piece
omitted for clarity)

Solid maple frame
1300 x 730 x 60 mm
(51³⁄₁₆ x 28¾ x 2⅜ in),
overlaps legs by 10 mm
(⅜ in) all around,
30 mm (1³⁄₁₆ in) thick

Drawer and
keyboard shelf
fronts made from
solid cherry

Cut-away view showing
hollow construction

Units set 20 mm
(¹³⁄₁₆ in) in from front

Back panel
Cherry pre-veneered MDF
1160 x 510 x 18 mm
(45¹¹⁄₁₆ x 20¹⁄₁₆ x ¹¹⁄₁₆ in),
set 100 mm (3¹⁵⁄₁₆ in) in from back

Side frame
660 mm high x
710 mm wide
(26 x 27¹⁵⁄₁₆ in)

Edging strips around
door are 5 mm (³⁄₁₆ in)
thick

DRAWER

Dowel joints

Solid pine

Plywood

Metal runner

DESK FRAME JOINT DETAIL

Mitre

Biscuit joint

Rebate
20 x 18 mm
(¹³⁄₁₆ x ¹¹⁄₁₆ in)

CABINET

572 mm
(22½ in)

280 mm (11 in)

Metal runner

Metal
shelf pegs

Edging strips
(on front edges)
5 mm (³⁄₁₆ in) thick

510 mm
(20¹⁄₁₆ in)

Computer

CROSS-SECTIONS OF KEYBOARD SHELF

Magnetic catch

Front of keyboard
shelf flaps down
(backflap hinge)

Metal runner

If putting a CPU in the cabinet, drill a hole for wires 60 mm (2⅜ in) in diameter
in the bottom of the cabinet at the back; another next to it and a third in the
side of the cabinet (near top, at back and hidden from view) for ventilation.
After installing, check that the CPU is adequately ventilated according to the
manufacturer's instructions. More ventilation may be necessary.

143

HOW TO MAKE THE WRITING DESK

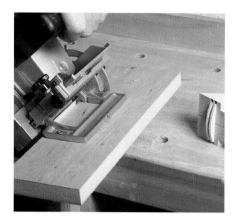

1 Making the mitred frames

The top and sides of the desk consist of a rebated, mitred frame into which pre-veneered boards are fitted. Cut the rebated frame pieces with the router and 15 mm (⅝ in) cutter or spindle moulder. Check that the depth of the rebate is fractionally greater than the thickness of the board. Mitre the ends and join with the biscuit jointer. Glue, clamp and check each frame for squareness.

2 Fitting the boards in the frames

When the frame joints are dry, cut, glue and clamp the veneered boards inside the frames; aim for a perfect fit. When the glue has dried, use the smoothing plane, followed by the cabinet scraper, to reduce the frame to the same level as the veneered boards. Take great care not to touch the veneer, as it is too thin to be planed and cannot tolerate much scraping. Sand lightly for a perfect flush finish.

3 Fixings and biscuit joints

Mark the location of the sides and back panel on the underside of the desktop. Mark the positions of the biscuit slots and the cam-dowel fixings. Transfer these locations to the sides and back panel. Cut the biscuit slots in the desktop and sides, and the cam-dowel holes in the desktop and back panel. The biscuit joints are for locating the desktop on the sides; they are not a permanent joint.

4 Making the cabinets

The two cabinets are made from cherry pre-veneered board, with plywood back panels, and are joined with glued biscuit joints. Drill holes for adjustable shelf pegs (to suit your requirements) before assembling the cabinets. Glue, clamp and check for squareness. Allow the glue to dry. Cut and fit the back panels (these can be simply face-fixed or set in rebates).

5 Making the doors, drawers and keyboard shelf

Cut the doors from cherry pre-veneered board and edge with strips of solid cherry. Trim and sand the edges flush with the board. Cut the drawer fronts and keyboard shelf front from solid cherry. Make the drawers from solid pine, using dowel joints (or dovetails), and cut and edge the keyboard shelf in the same way as for the doors. The shelves need only be edged on the front edge.

6 Assembling the top, sides and back

You may need help to assemble the desk. Place the desktop upside down on a soft surface (such as carpeted floor). Fit the sides to the backboard. Lower the sides and backboard on to the fixings and biscuits on the desktop. Tighten the cam-dowel fixings all the way around.

7 Fixing the cabinets

Fix the cabinets to the desk using screws entered through the top and side of the cabinet. Fit the drawer runners and catches to the cabinets. Turn the desk the right way up and fit the drawers. When everything fits well, disassemble and sand all surfaces clean and smooth.

8 Finishing

Apply an oil and wax finish (or sprayed lacquer if you have that option) to the components before reassembling. Apply one thin coat of oil with a soft cloth; do not use an excessive amount because it will result in a streaky finish. Allow to dry and remove roughness with the finest sandpaper. Apply a second coat of oil, allow to dry and smooth with wire wool. Apply wax polish. Reassemble.

BOOKCASE

You can never have enough shelves, that's for certain. And shelves are even more useful if they are adjustable. This bookcase is made from solid oak and oak pre-veneered MDF. The four little drawers are ideally suited for CDs, or perfect for tidying away odds and ends.

YOU WILL NEED

- Table saw, planer and thicknesser (or buy prepared wood)
- Sliding compound mitre saw
- Bandsaw
- Router, router table, 5 mm (³⁄₁₆ in) and 10 mm (³⁄₈ in) straight cutters
- Crosshead screwdrivers
- Cordless driver, screwdriver bit, and twist bits to suit shelf pegs and fixings
- Orbital sander, sanding block and 80-grit and 600-grit sandpaper
- Block plane
- Spokeshave
- Pencil, ruler, tape measure and try square
- Four sash clamps
- Iron
- Wood: see drawing – oak, oak pre-veneered MDF, MDF, oak-faced plywood and oak iron-on veneer edging strip
- Cam-dowel fixings: 16
- Fluted dowels: 2
- Knobs of your choice
- Shelf pegs to suit your requirements
- Plugs and screws for fixing bookcase to the wall
- Expansion plates: 4
- PVA glue, water and cloth
- Finishing oil and wax
- Oiling and polishing cloths

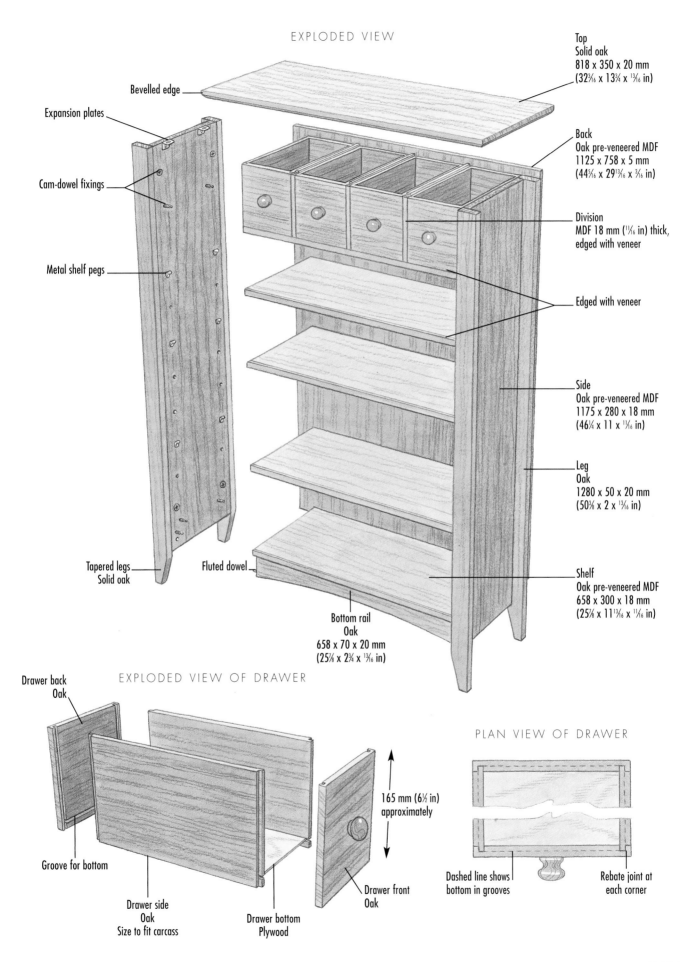

EXPLODED VIEW

Bevelled edge

Expansion plates

Cam-dowel fixings

Metal shelf pegs

Tapered legs
Solid oak

Top
Solid oak
818 x 350 x 20 mm
(32³⁄₁₆ x 13¾ x ¹³⁄₁₆ in)

Back
Oak pre-veneered MDF
1125 x 758 x 5 mm
(44⁵⁄₁₆ x 29¹³⁄₁₆ x ³⁄₁₆ in)

Division
MDF 18 mm (¹¹⁄₁₆ in) thick,
edged with veneer

Edged with veneer

Side
Oak pre-veneered MDF
1175 x 280 x 18 mm
(46¼ x 11 x ¹¹⁄₁₆ in)

Leg
Oak
1280 x 50 x 20 mm
(50³⁄₈ x 2 x ¹³⁄₁₆ in)

Shelf
Oak pre-veneered MDF
658 x 300 x 18 mm
(25⁷⁄₈ x 11¹³⁄₁₆ x ¹¹⁄₁₆ in)

Fluted dowel

Bottom rail
Oak
658 x 70 x 20 mm
(25⁷⁄₈ x 2¾ x ¹³⁄₁₆ in)

EXPLODED VIEW OF DRAWER

Drawer back
Oak

Groove for bottom

Drawer side
Oak
Size to fit carcass

Drawer bottom
Plywood

165 mm (6½ in)
approximately

Drawer front
Oak

PLAN VIEW OF DRAWER

Dashed line shows
bottom in grooves

Rebate joint at
each corner

147

HOW TO MAKE THE BOOKCASE

1 Preparing the wood

Cut and plane the legs to the finished size. Prepare the rails, leaving them longer than needed; use the try square to check that the edges are square to the faces. Cut the sides and back from pre-veneered MDF, taking care not to damage the edges of the veneer. Mark the tapers on the bottoms of the legs, cut them with the bandsaw and plane smooth.

2 Shaping the bottom rail

Mark out the curve on the bottom rail. The curve should look smooth and symmetrical: plan out one half on a piece of paper, then cut it out and use it as a template to draw around, flipping it over to mark out the other half of the curve. Cut the curve on the bandsaw and use the spokeshave to smooth the edge.

3 Joining the MDF boards to the legs

The MDF boards are joined to the legs with cam-dowel joints, and the legs are joined to the rails with cam-dowels and wooden dowels. Mark the location of the holes for the cams and dowels, then drill them. Assemble the structure and check that it is square. Take it apart and sand the legs and rails smooth.

4 Edging the boards

The edges of the pre-veneered MDF boards require edging. We have used pre-glued veneer edging that is ironed on, but you could also use solid wood lipping of 5 mm (³⁄₁₆ in) thickness or more. Centre the veneer strip on the edge, press down hard with the hot iron and follow immediately with a block of wood, rubbing the block back and forth to fix the veneer as the glue bond cools down.

6 Cutting the grooves in the drawer bottom

Reset the router table with the 5 mm (³⁄₁₆ in) straight cutter and cut grooves right through the sides, front and back of the drawers.

5 Cutting the housing joints for the drawers

The drawers are held together with housing joints. Set up the router in the router table, fitted with the 5 mm (³⁄₁₆ in) straight cutter. Cut right through the front and back of the drawers to produce a housing groove as shown above. Reset the router with the 10 mm (³⁄₈ in) straight cutter for rebating the sides. Practise on a scrap of wood of the same thickness to achieve a tightly fitting joint.

8 Finishing

Plane the top, sides and base of the drawers (if uneven); sand with the orbital sander. Assemble the carcass. Fit the top on using expansion plates. Use the fluted dowels to reinforce the cam-dowel joints between the bottom rail and the sides. Check that the drawers fit and make adjustments. Make the shelves, edged with iron-on veneer. They should fit loosely. Apply two coats of finishing oil followed by one coat of wax polish. Fit the drawer knobs.

7 Gluing the drawers together

Cut bottoms for the drawers: measure the length and width based on the grooves you have cut. Make the bottoms fractionally smaller than these dimensions so that they do not prevent the drawer joints from closing up. Practise clamping before you apply the glue (use offcuts to prevent the clamps marking the wood). Check that the drawer is square and allow the glue to dry.

DINING TABLE AND CHAIR

This dining suite looks like it has come right out of a Van Gogh painting. Simple shapes and chunky proportions typify this rustic style. It is made entirely from knotty pine (the kind you can buy in your local DIY store in ready-prepared sections), but you could use knot-free pine. If you prefer hardwood, you will probably need to slim down the sections throughout to reduce their weight. The tapering shapes are easy to make, but the shaved back slats and whittled "acorns" are a little more challenging.

YOU WILL NEED

- Table saw, planer and thicknesser (or buy prepared wood)
- Sliding compound mitre saw
- Bandsaw
- Smoothing plane
- Spokeshave
- Mortiser, 15 mm ($^{19}/_{16}$ in) and 10 mm ($^3/_8$ in) mortise chisels
- Chisel
- Rubber mallet
- Crosshead screwdrivers
- Cordless driver, screwdriver bit, and twist bits to suit screws
- Orbital sander, 80-grit and 600-grit sandpaper
- Pencil, ruler, tape measure and try square
- Four sash clamps
- Forstner drill bit: 25 mm (1 in)
- Sharp knife for whittling
- Wood: see drawing – pine and pine dowelling
- Screws: No. 8 cross-headed, zinc-plated, countersink: 16 x 25 mm (1 in); 8 x 38 mm (1½ in)
- Expansion plates: 12, with 15 mm ($^{19}/_{16}$ in) screws
- PVA glue, water and cloth
- Varnish
- Brushes

TABLE: GENERAL VIEW

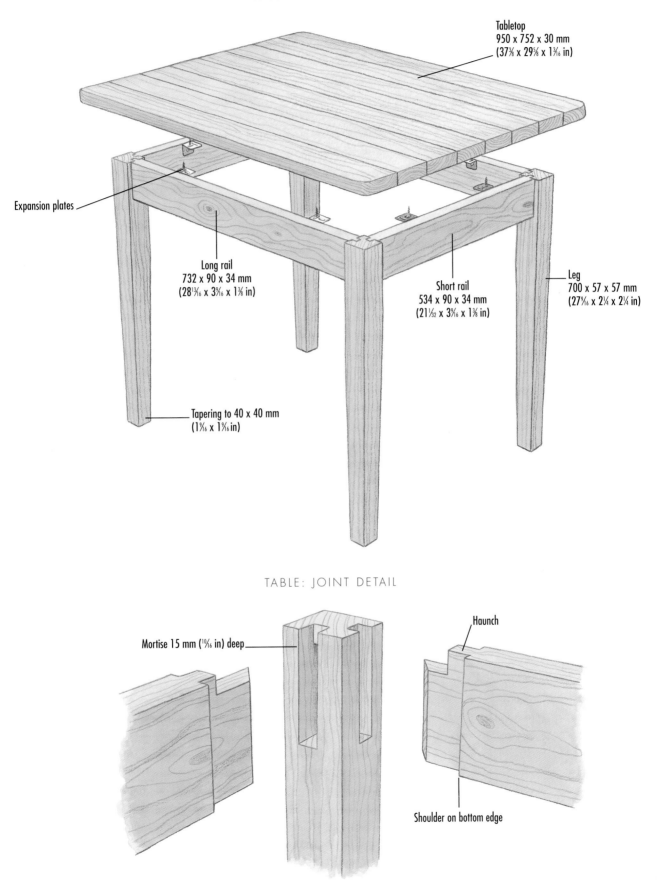

Tabletop
950 x 752 x 30 mm
(37⅜ x 29⅝ x 1³⁄₁₆ in)

Expansion plates

Long rail
732 x 90 x 34 mm
(28¹³⁄₁₆ x 3⁹⁄₁₆ x 1⅜ in)

Short rail
534 x 90 x 34 mm
(21¹⁄₃₂ x 3⁹⁄₁₆ x 1⅜ in)

Leg
700 x 57 x 57 mm
(27⁹⁄₁₆ x 2¼ x 2¼ in)

Tapering to 40 x 40 mm
(1⁹⁄₁₆ x 1⁹⁄₁₆ in)

TABLE: JOINT DETAIL

Mortise 15 mm (¹⁰⁄₁₆ in) deep

Haunch

Shoulder on bottom edge

HOW TO MAKE THE DINING TABLE

1 Cutting the mortises

Mark out the positions of the mortises on the tops of the legs. Cut these out by hand using a drill bit, chisel and mallet, or use a mortiser. If you are using a mortiser, you may achieve a better result if you leave the legs over-length and cut the mortise including the area for the haunch, before cutting it to the finished length. Clean out the mortise corners with the chisel.

2 Cutting the tenons

Cut tenons on the ends of the rails to correspond with the mortises in the legs. Mitre the ends of the tenons on the compound mitre saw. When the rails are fitted into the legs, the mitred ends of the tenons must not touch, as this may prevent the shoulders of the joints from closing up properly. Shave off excess wood to achieve a good fit.

3 Tapering the legs

Mark the tapered shape on the sides of the legs. Double-check that you are tapering the insides of the legs (sawing material away from the same side as the tenon is cut). Cut away the bulk of the waste with the bandsaw and use the smoothing plane to flatten and smooth the surfaces.

4 Assembling the frame

Check that each joint fits correctly and make adjustments as necessary; use a chisel to shave away excess wood. Set the clamps to the correct length and prepare waste blocks for protecting the work. It is best to clamp in two stages: firstly, glue the legs to the short rails and wait for the glue to dry; and secondly, join these two frames with the long rails as shown above.

5 Making the tabletop

Cut lengths of wood for making the tabletop. Leave them about 25 mm (1 in) longer than needed so that you can cut the top to the finished length once the glue has dried. Set the clamps to the correct length and arrange the lengths of wood so that the curves in the end grain alternate: upward and downward. When dry, cut to size, sand and fit to the frame. Finish the table with varnish.

CHAIR: SIDE VIEW

1 square = 50 mm (2 in)

890 x 98 x 45 mm
(35¹⁄₁₆ x 3⅞ x 1¾ in)

Seat rail
316 (plus tenons) x 60 x 30 mm
(12⁷⁄₁₆ x 2⅜ x 1³⁄₁₆ in)

Leg
400 x 45 x 45 mm
(15¾ x 1¾ x 1¾ in)

Stretcher
Dowelling 25 mm (1 in)
in diameter, cut to fit

CHAIR: BACK SLAT

1 square = 25 mm (1 in)

CHAIR: SEAT

Notched to fit

427 x 380 x 18 mm
(16¹³⁄₁₆ x 14¹⁵⁄₁₆ x ¹¹⁄₁₆ in)

CHAIR: PLAN VIEW

Corner block
115 x 50 x 42 mm
(4½ x 2 x 1¾ in)

CHAIR: EXPLODED VIEW

Assemble side
frames first

Stretcher
Dowelling 25 mm (1 in)
in diameter, cut to fit

CHAIR: FRONT VIEW

Whittled acorns

Back slat
280 (plus tenons)
x 50 x 27 mm
(11 x 2 x ¹¹⁄₁₆ in)

Seat rail
280 (plus tenons)
x 60 x 30 mm
(11 x 2⅜ x 1³⁄₁₆ in)

153

HOW TO MAKE THE DINING CHAIR

1 Shaping the legs

The legs are tapered as shown in the drawing, but it is best to mortise and drill the legs beforehand. Mark the tapers and the mortise joints on the sides of the legs. Cut out the mortises on the mortiser and clean the corners of the joints with a chisel. Drill the holes for the dowelling in the legs with the forstner bit. Cut the tapers on the bandsaw and plane and shave them smooth as shown above.

2 Acorns, rails and stretchers

The upper part of the back legs forms the uprights of the seat back of the chair. Use a sharp knife to whittle the acorn shapes on the top of them. Leave them textured, or sand smooth. Prepare the seat rails and cut tenons on the ends (the joints are similar to the table tenons opposite). Cut lengths of dowelling for the stretchers.

3 Back slats

Use the grid on the drawing to plot the shape of the back slats. Cut out the shape on the bandsaw, as close to the outline as possible. The ends of the slats do not have tenons with shoulders, so they need to be an accurate, slightly wedged fit in the mortises. Asssemble the chair without glue and check that the slats fit. Plane them with the spokeshave. Sand all components smooth.

4 Assembling

Check that all the joints close up correctly before gluing them together. Make sure you have set the clamps to the correct length and have protective blocks ready. Glue and clamp the two side frames independently, check for squareness and allow to dry. Join the two side frames with the remaining rails and stretchers, as shown above.

5 Making the corner blocks

Cut corner blocks on the compound mitre saw (set at 45°) and screw them to the frame – these reinforce the structure.

6 Completing the chair

Make the seat slab by gluing together lengths of wood in the same way as you did for the tabletop. Mark and cut the notches at the back to accommodate the legs, and sand smooth. Fit the seat to the frame using four expansion plates. Sand for a second time and finish with varnish.

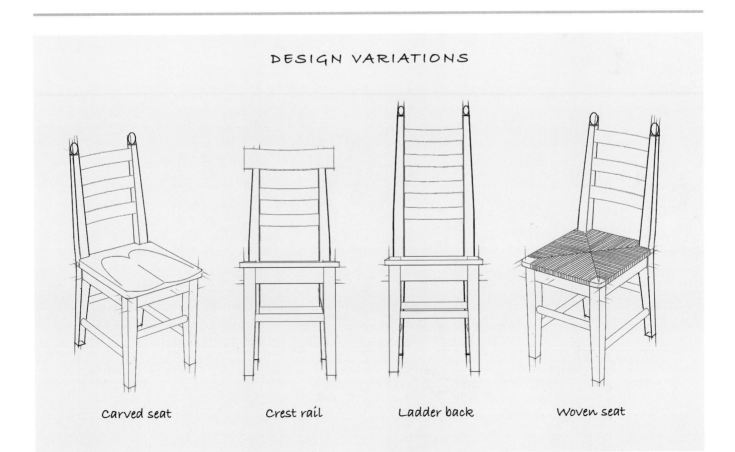

DESIGN VARIATIONS

Carved seat   Crest rail   Ladder back   Woven seat

WAVE CABINET

Acoustic vibrations were the inspiration for this CD and DVD cabinet, or rippling soundwaves at least! This is a time-consuming project, which requires many evenings spent gluing up laminated wavy shapes, but the results are worth it: a curvaceous one-off that is sure to grab people's attention and attract some compliments. The doors are each made from seven identical panels consisting of layers of plywood topped with cherry veneer. So, show off your woodworking skills by making this laminated beauty.

YOU WILL NEED

- Table saw, planer and thicknesser (or buy prepared wood)
- Sliding compound mitre saw
- Bandsaw
- Router and 10 mm (⅜ in) straight cutter with a guide bearing at the tip
- Spokeshave
- Smoothing plane and block plane
- Crosshead screwdriver
- Cordless driver, screwdriver bit, and twist bits to suit dowels, shelf pegs and fixings
- Orbital sander, 80-grit and 600-grit sandpaper
- Pencil, ruler, tape measure and try square
- Three sash clamps and six G-clamps
- Iron
- Wood: see drawing – maple, birch plywood, maple iron-on edging veneer, cherry veneer; offcuts for former
- Door hinges of your choice: 6, with screws
- Knobs and catches of your choice
- Shelf pegs to suit your requirements
- Fluted dowels: 48 x 6 mm (¼ in); 16 x 8 mm (⁵⁄₁₆ in) for feet
- Cam-dowels: 8
- Plugs and screws for fixing to wall
- PVA glue, water and cloth
- Paper for lining former
- Finishing oil and wax
- Oiling and polishing cloths

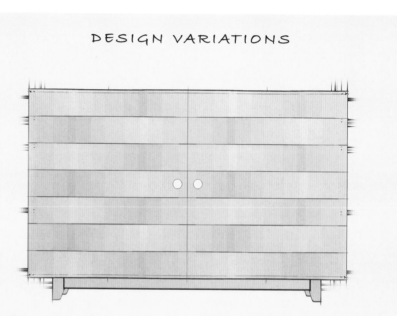

DESIGN VARIATIONS

Longer unit with rails underneath

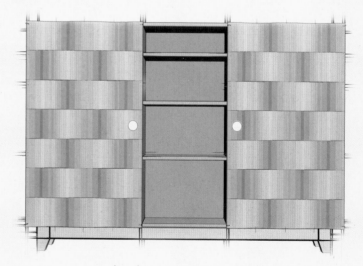

Longer unit with open shelves in the middle

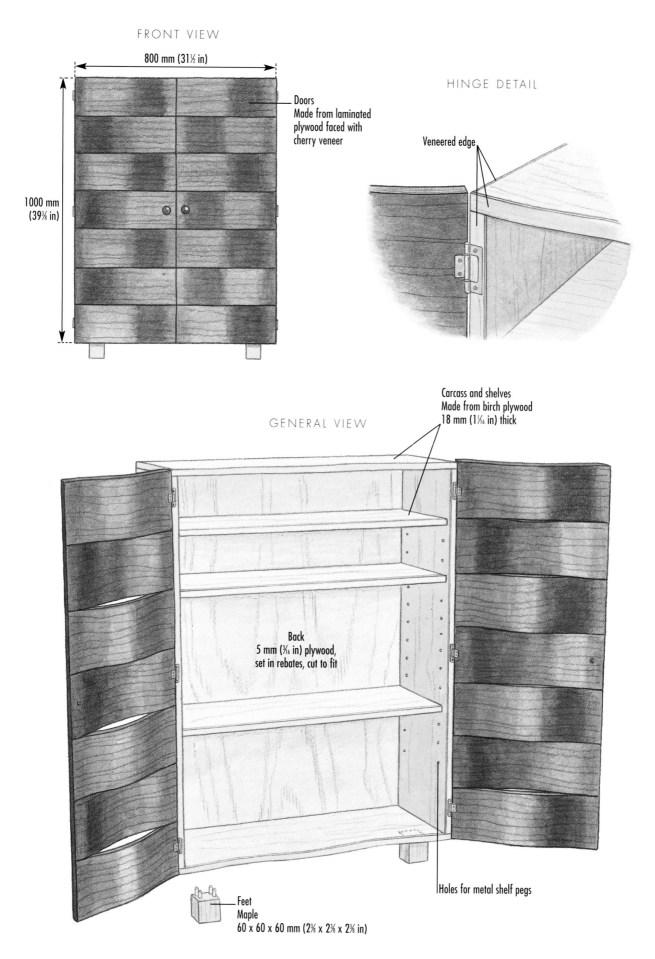

FRONT VIEW

800 mm (31½ in)

1000 mm
(39⅜ in)

Doors
Made from laminated
plywood faced with
cherry veneer

HINGE DETAIL

Veneered edge

Carcass and shelves
Made from birch plywood
18 mm (1⅟₁₆ in) thick

GENERAL VIEW

Back
5 mm (³⁄₁₆ in) plywood,
set in rebates, cut to fit

Holes for metal shelf pegs

Feet
Maple
60 x 60 x 60 mm (2⅜ x 2⅜ x 2⅜ in)

PLAN VIEW

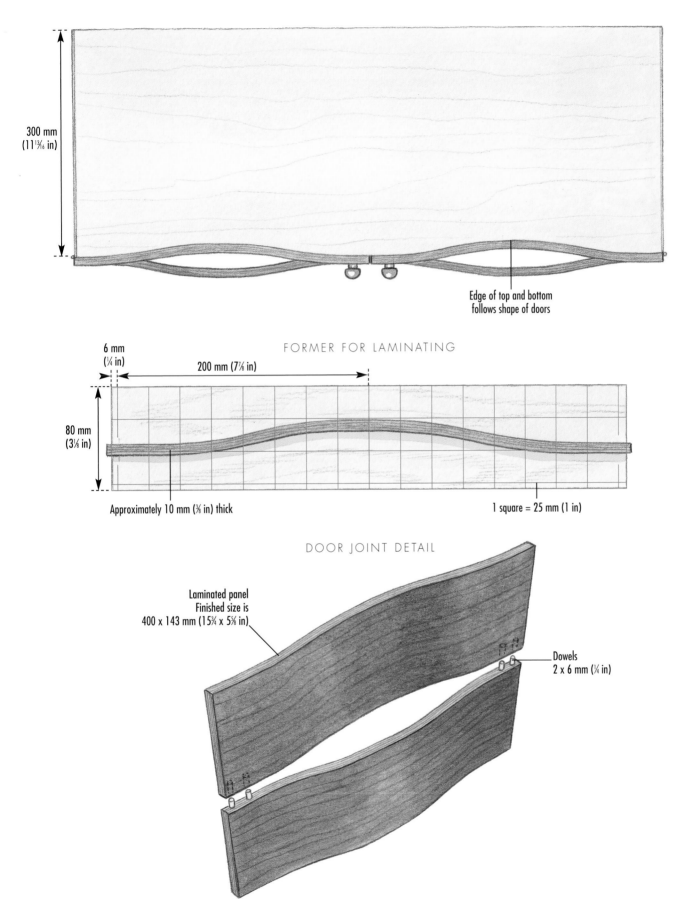

300 mm
(11¹³⁄₁₆ in)

Edge of top and bottom
follows shape of doors

FORMER FOR LAMINATING

6 mm
(¼ in)

200 mm (7⅞ in)

80 mm
(3⅛ in)

Approximately 10 mm (⅜ in) thick

1 square = 25 mm (1 in)

DOOR JOINT DETAIL

Laminated panel
Finished size is
400 x 143 mm (15¾ x 5⅝ in)

Dowels
2 x 6 mm (¼ in)

HOW TO MAKE THE WAVE CABINET

1 Making the original curved shapes of the former from offcuts

Use the grid on the drawing as a guide to plotting out one side of the curved shape on a piece of wood. Calculate the thickness of the lamination by stacking the layers (1 paper, 1 veneer, 2 plywood, 1 veneer, 1 paper). Mark this thickness at intervals of 10 mm (⅜ in) or so to one side of the curve. Draw a smooth curve through these points. Cut out the two curved shapes and smooth with a spokeshave.

2 Duplicating the shapes

The curved shapes need to be duplicated and stacked together to make a former that is a solid block of nine shapes. Draw around the originals and cut out the shapes, leaving about 1–2 mm (½₂–⅟₁₆ in) extra material all around. Make a baseboard with dowels as shown, drill location holes in all pieces and use the router and bearing-tipped cutter to trace around the original shapes.

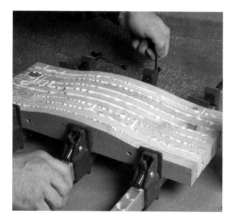

3 Gluing the former together

Arrange the clamps and practise clamping the shapes together to make the two halves of the former. When you are ready, apply glue and reclamp. Check that the block is square and flat (the pieces may slip out of position) and make adjustments as necessary. Wipe off excess glue with a damp cloth.

4 Laminating

Add scraps of plywood to one half of the former as shown to prevent things slipping. Prepare the door panels: 1 layer paper, 1 layer veneer, 2 layers plywood, 1 layer veneer, 1 layer paper. Place the glued layers, with paper either side, in the former. Tighten the central and then the side clamps.

5 Trimming the door panels

It is important that the curved panels are perfectly square and identical in size. Start by planing one of the long edges flat and smooth. Use the bandsaw and parallel fence to remove the waste on the other long side. Plane down to the finished width and check that the edges are parallel. Cut off the ends with the compound mitre saw.

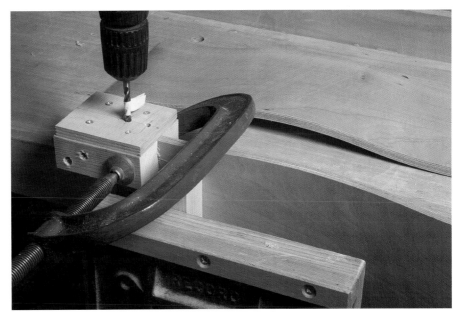

6 Making the dowel joints in the door panels

Make a simple drilling jig from wood and scraps of plywood as shown above: this guides the drill and produces holes in the same position each time. Use the same jig at each corner and for all the curved panels (the top and bottom panels of each door do not need drilling in the top and bottom sides). Glue and clamp the doors, checking that they remain rigid.

7 Making the carcass

The carcass is made from plywood joined with cam-dowel fixings. Mark out the wavy front edges of the top and bottom pieces (use a door as a template) and cut out on the bandsaw (keep the waste for clamping on the edging veneer). Glue strips of edging veneer to the exposed plywood edges of the carcass and shelves. Mark the locations of the cam-dowels and drill the holes.

8 Completing the cabinet

Drill holes for the adjustable shelving – to suit your requirements. Make feet with bevelled edges as shown. Fix the feet to the bottom panel of the cabinet with four dowels. Assemble the cabinet and hang the doors. Fit the handle and catches. Disassemble, sand the surfaces smooth and round over sharp edges. Apply an oil and wax finish, and reassemble.

KITCHEN UNITS

Kitchen design has come a long way over the years and you might think it's not worth making your own units, but remember all the dilapidated fitted kitchens you have seen, which have worn out in less than five years. Cheap materials and veneered or gloss-lacquered finishes do not last long in a kitchen environment, so there is a good argument for making your own units from more sturdy materials. You may wish to adjust the dimensions to incorporate an oven or a fridge.

YOU WILL NEED

- Table saw, planer and thicknesser (or buy prepared wood)
- Router and 5 mm (³⁄₁₆ in) straight cutter
- Sliding compound mitre saw
- Mortiser, 15 mm (⅝ in) and 10 mm (⅜ in) mortise chisels
- Crosshead screwdriver
- Cordless driver, screwdriver bit, twist bits to suit shelf pegs and fixings, and countersink bit for No. 8 screws
- Electric drill, combination bit (drills a counterbored clearance hole and pilot hole) and plug-cutter set to suit No. 8 screws
- Pillar drill
- Orbital sander, 80-grit and 600-grit sandpaper
- Chisel
- Pencil, ruler, tape measure, spirit level and try square
- Sash clamps
- Wood: see drawing – plywood, pine and moulding
- Pins: 15 mm (⅝ in)
- Screws: No. 8 cross-headed, zinc-plated, countersink: 50 mm (2 in); 25 mm (1 in)
- Drawer runners
- Plugs, screws and brackets for fixing units to floor and wall
- Hinges, handles, catches, shelf pegs
- Tiles, tile adhesive and grout
- PVA glue, water and cloth
- Paint and brushes

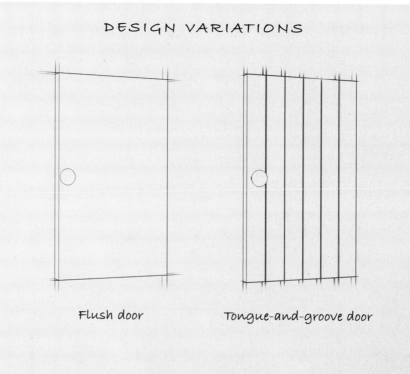

DESIGN VARIATIONS

Flush door

Tongue-and-groove door

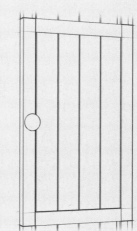

Frame and tongue-and-grooved panel door

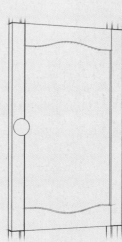

Decorative frame and panel door

SURFACE

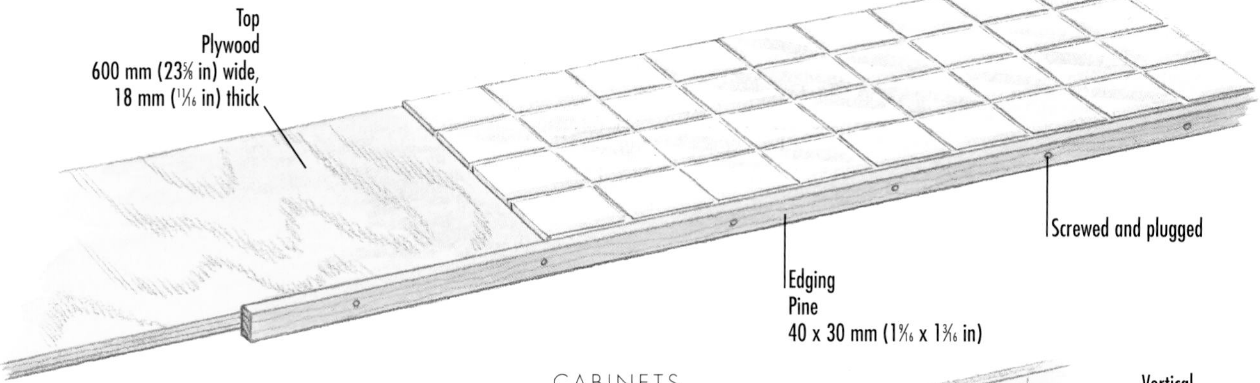
Top
Plywood
600 mm (23 5/8 in) wide,
18 mm (11/16 in) thick
Screwed and plugged
Edging
Pine
40 x 30 mm (1 9/16 x 1 3/16 in)

CABINETS

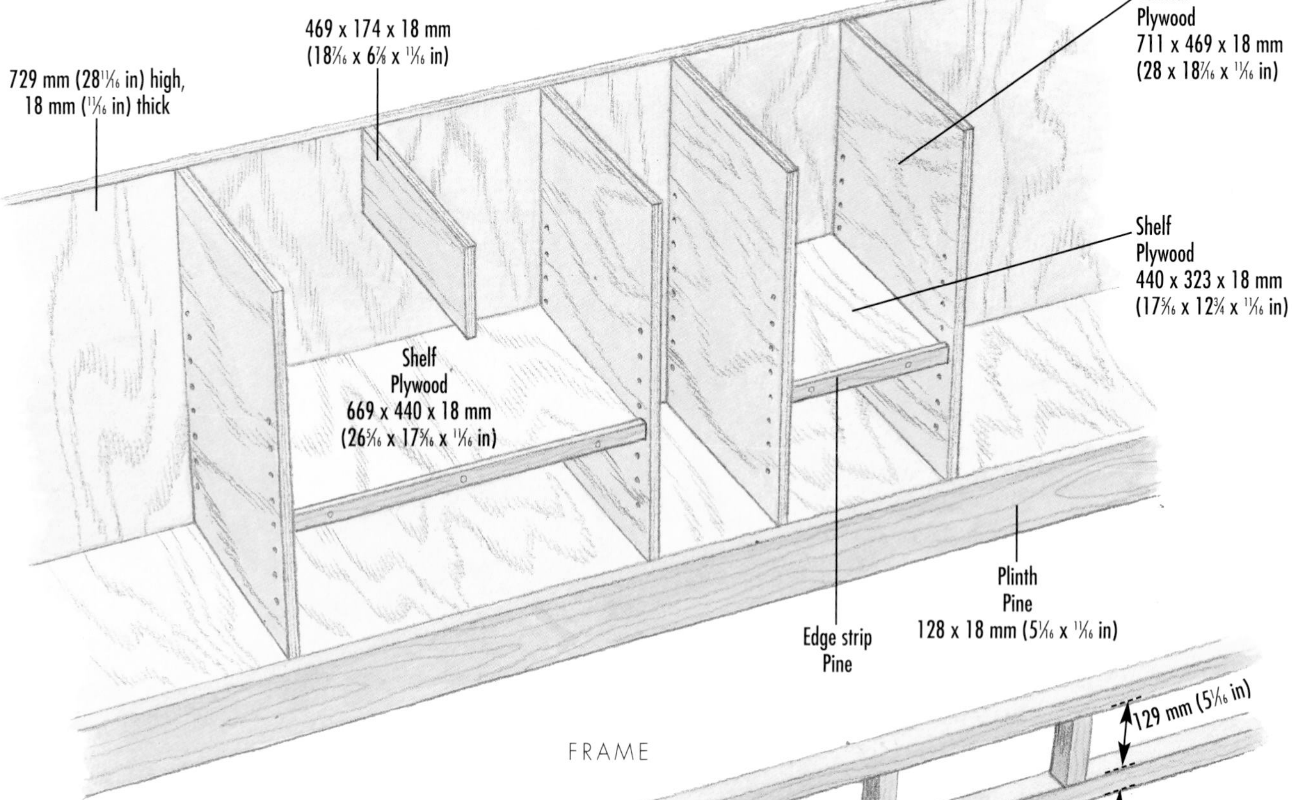
469 x 174 x 18 mm
(18 7/16 x 6 7/8 x 11/16 in)
729 mm (28 11/16 in) high,
18 mm (11/16 in) thick
Vertical
Plywood
711 x 469 x 18 mm
(28 x 18 7/16 x 11/16 in)
Shelf
Plywood
440 x 323 x 18 mm
(17 5/16 x 12 3/4 x 11/16 in)
Shelf
Plywood
669 x 440 x 18 mm
(26 5/16 x 17 5/16 x 11/16 in)
Plinth
Pine
128 x 18 mm (5 1/16 x 11/16 in)
Edge strip
Pine

FRAME

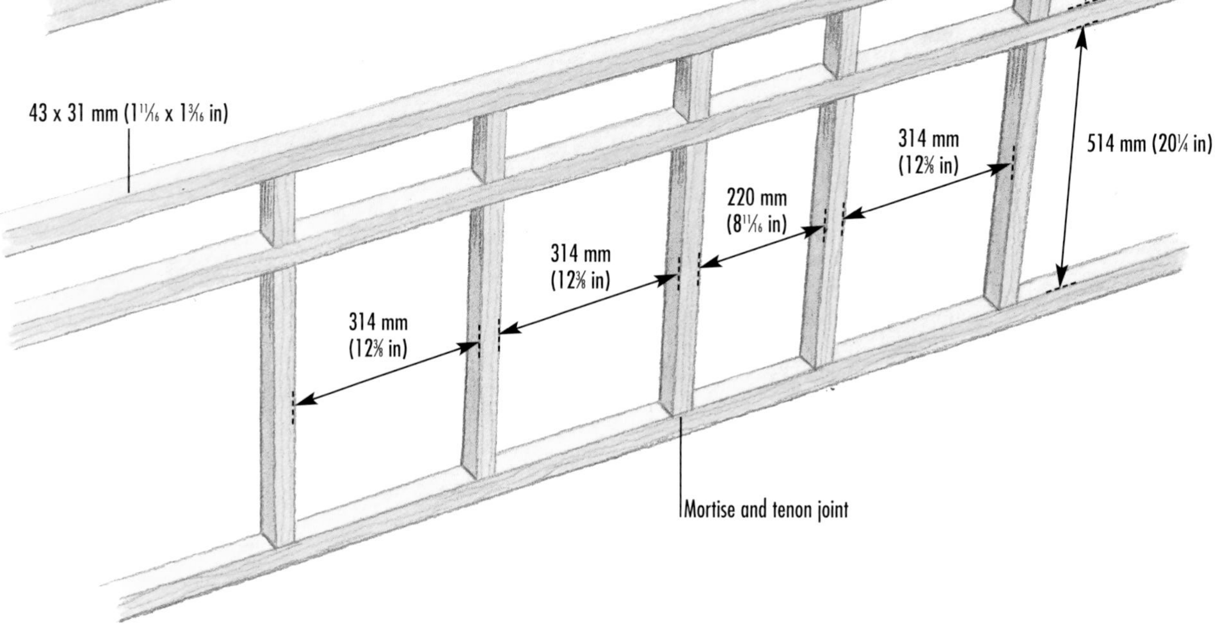
129 mm (5 1/16 in)
43 x 31 mm (1 11/16 x 1 3/16 in)
314 mm
(12 3/8 in)
514 mm (20 1/4 in)
220 mm
(8 11/16 in)
314 mm
(12 3/8 in)
314 mm
(12 3/8 in)
Mortise and tenon joint

FRONT VIEW

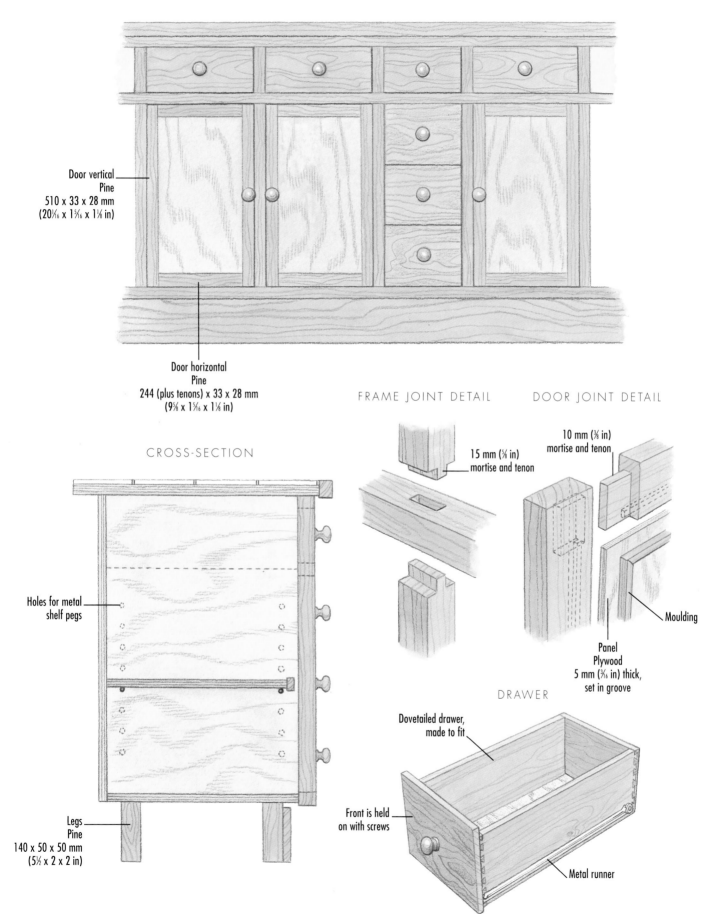

Door vertical
Pine
510 x 33 x 28 mm
(20⅟₁₆ x 1⁵⁄₁₆ x 1⅛ in)

Door horizontal
Pine
244 (plus tenons) x 33 x 28 mm
(9⅝ x 1⁵⁄₁₆ x 1⅛ in)

FRAME JOINT DETAIL

15 mm (⅝ in)
mortise and tenon

DOOR JOINT DETAIL

10 mm (⅜ in)
mortise and tenon

Moulding

Panel
Plywood
5 mm (³⁄₁₆ in) thick,
set in groove

CROSS-SECTION

Holes for metal
shelf pegs

Legs
Pine
140 x 50 x 50 mm
(5½ x 2 x 2 in)

DRAWER

Dovetailed drawer,
made to fit

Front is held
on with screws

Metal runner

HOW TO MAKE THE KITCHEN UNITS

1 Legs and base

Cut legs of the same length and mark their positions on the baseboard. Set them in from the front and ends by the same amount all around (the plinth is fixed to the legs later on). Space the legs at intervals of approximately 500 mm (19¹¹⁄₁₆ in), but avoid placing them beneath a vertical board. Fix the legs to the baseboard with glue and screws.

2 Fixing the vertical boards

The vertical boards form the sides of the cabinets and are identical to each other. Before assembling these verticals, drill holes in them for the adjustable shelf pegs, at intervals to suit your requirements. Mark the location of the verticals on the baseboard, put in position and fix with 50 mm (2 in) screws.

3 Fixing the top

Mark out the locations of the verticals on the top of the cabinets. These should correspond with those on the baseboard.

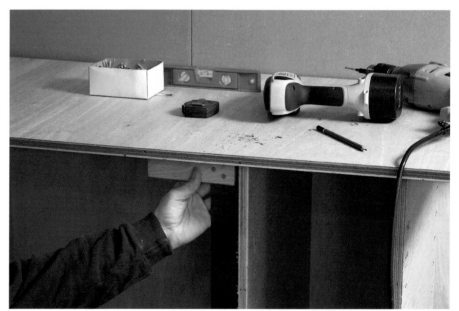

4 Completing the cabinets

Push the cabinets against the wall in their final position. Use the spirit level and wedges under the legs to level the unit. Secure the legs to the floor. Locate the top and check the positions of the verticals with the try square. Screw the top to the verticals. Secure the top to the wall using concealed brackets.

5 Making the front frame

Mark out the lengths of wood for the front frame, and mark the mortises and tenons. Cut the mortises on the mortiser and clean out the corners of the joints with the chisel. Cut the tenons on the compound mitre saw. Practise cutting a tenon on a scrap of wood of the same section to check that the settings are correct. Glue and clamp the frame and check that it is flat and square.

6 Fixing the front frame

Drill counterbored holes in the front of the frame for receiving screws that can later be concealed with plugs of solid wood. Hold the frame in the correct position on the front of the unit (check with a spirit level) and drill the holes with a combination drill bit (one that drills a counterbored hole, a clearance hole and a pilot hole at the same time). Screw in place and plug the holes.

7 Making the doors

Cut verticals that are slightly over-length. Make the mortise and tenon joints and cut the grooves for the panel with the router and 5 mm (³⁄₁₆ in) straight cutter. Cut the panel to fit inside the frame. Practise clamping the door and then glue, clamp and check that the door is square. Cut and plane the joints at the corners.

8 Making the drawers

Make drawers using dovetail joints as shown on page 113. Fit the fronts on to the drawers using 25 mm (1 in) countersunk screws. Make shelves. Fit the drawer runners. Hang the doors. Fit the door and drawer handles and door catches. Tile the top. Fix the edging to the top and the plinth to the feet. Sand everything with the orbital sander and apply a paint finish.

167

FOLDING CHAIR

It is always useful to have more space, so folding chairs might be the ideal solution for your living/dining area. This solid maple and laminated birch design folds away to a slender upright shape for leaning against a wall (or it can be hung on the wall if you drill a hole in the back). Both the seat and the back are curved in two directions, which makes this interesting from a laminating perspective. We have made things easier by using two layers of plywood instead of using constructional veneer.

YOU WILL NEED

- Table saw, planer and thicknesser (or buy prepared wood)
- Sliding compound mitre saw
- Bandsaw
- Router and 5 mm (³⁄₁₆ in) straight cutter
- Mortiser; 10 mm (⅜ in) mortise chisel
- Crosshead screwdriver
- Cordless driver, screwdriver bit, twist bits to suit screws, and combination bit (drills a counterbored clearance hole and pilot hole) and plug-cutter set to suit No. 8 screws and screwdriver bit
- Pillar drill and 6.5 mm (¼ in) twist bit
- Orbital sander, 80-grit and 600-grit sandpaper
- Smoothing plane and block plane
- Chisel
- Spokeshave
- Pencil, ruler, tape measure, try square
- Six sash clamps and one fast-clamp
- Wood: see drawing – maple and plywood
- Stainless-steel plate
- Screws: No. 8 cross-headed, zinc-plated, countersink: 75 x 50 mm (2 in); 14 x 20 mm (1³⁄₁₆ in); 100 x 15 mm (⅝ in)
- Hex key bolts 6 mm (¼ in) in diameter: 4 x 35 mm (1⅜ in) long (A) and (C) 2 x 50 mm (2 in) long (B); 8 washers and 6 pronged T-nuts to fit
- PVA glue, water and cloth
- Varnish and wax polish
- Brushes and polishing cloths

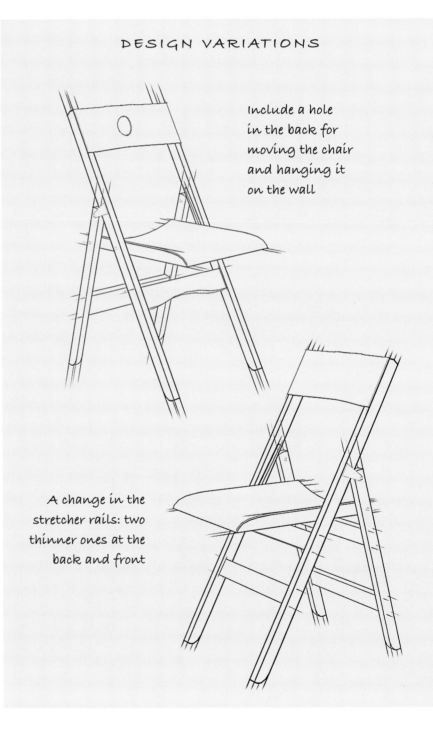

DESIGN VARIATIONS

Include a hole in the back for moving the chair and hanging it on the wall

A change in the stretcher rails: two thinner ones at the back and front

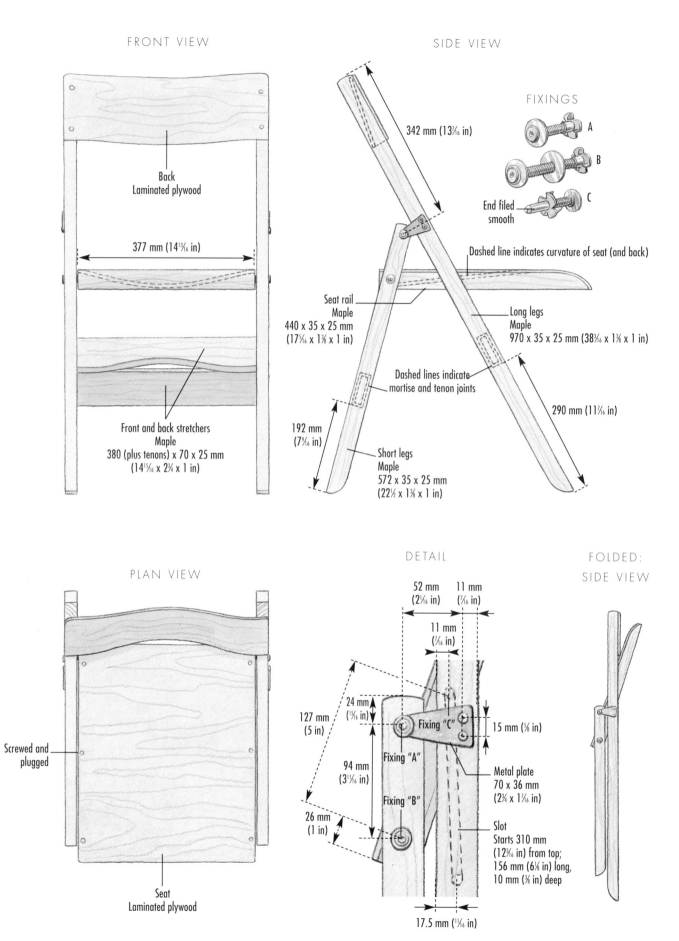

FRONT VIEW

Back
Laminated plywood

377 mm (14¹³⁄₁₆ in)

Front and back stretchers
Maple
380 (plus tenons) x 70 x 25 mm
(14¹⁵⁄₁₆ x 2¾ x 1 in)

SIDE VIEW

342 mm (13⁷⁄₁₆ in)

FIXINGS

A

B

C
End filed
smooth

Dashed line indicates curvature of seat (and back)

Seat rail
Maple
440 x 35 x 25 mm
(17⁵⁄₁₆ x 1⅜ x 1 in)

Long legs
Maple
970 x 35 x 25 mm (38³⁄₁₆ x 1⅜ x 1 in)

Dashed lines indicate
mortise and tenon joints

192 mm
(7⁹⁄₁₆ in)

290 mm (11⁷⁄₁₆ in)

Short legs
Maple
572 x 35 x 25 mm
(22½ x 1⅜ x 1 in)

PLAN VIEW

Screwed and
plugged

Seat
Laminated plywood

DETAIL

52 mm
(2¹⁄₁₆ in)

11 mm
(⁷⁄₁₆ in)

11 mm
(⁷⁄₁₆ in)

127 mm
(5 in)

24 mm
(¹⁵⁄₁₆ in)

Fixing "C"

15 mm (⅝ in)

Fixing "A"

94 mm
(3¹¹⁄₁₆ in)

Metal plate
70 x 36 mm
(2¾ x 1⁷⁄₁₆ in)

Fixing "B"

26 mm
(1 in)

Slot
Starts 310 mm
(12³⁄₁₆ in) from top;
156 mm (6⅛ in) long,
10 mm (⅜ in) deep

17.5 mm (¹¹⁄₁₆ in)

FOLDED:
SIDE VIEW

BACK FORMER: EXPLODED VIEW

480 x 208 x 25 mm
(18⅛ x 8³⁄₁₆ x 1 in)

DETAIL

Seat is curved
at the back

The smoothed end of
fixing "C" runs in this slot

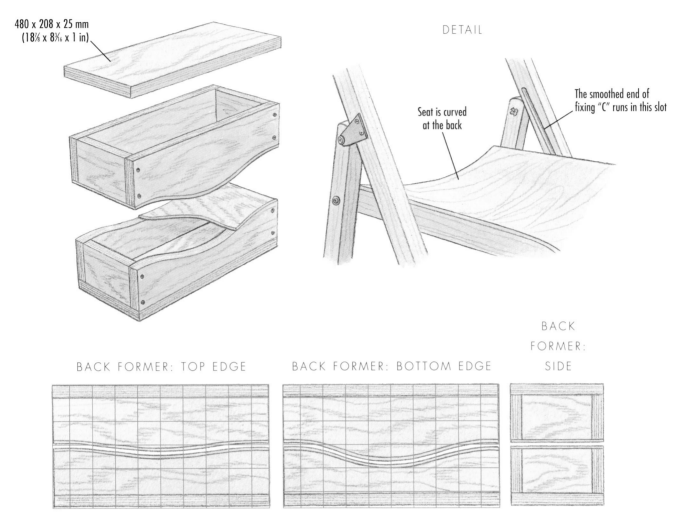

BACK FORMER: TOP EDGE

BACK FORMER: BOTTOM EDGE

BACK FORMER: SIDE

SEAT FORMER: EXPLODED VIEW

440 mm
(17⁵⁄₁₆ in)

495 mm
(19½ in)

105 mm
(4⅛ in)

SEAT FORMER: SIDE VIEW

SEAT FORMER: FRONT VIEW

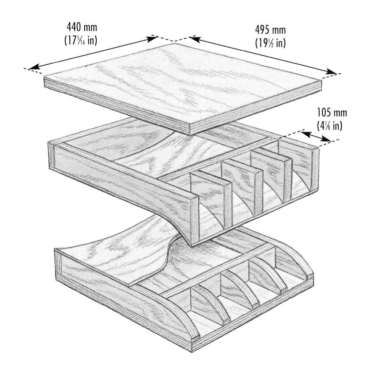

171

HOW TO MAKE THE FOLDING CHAIR

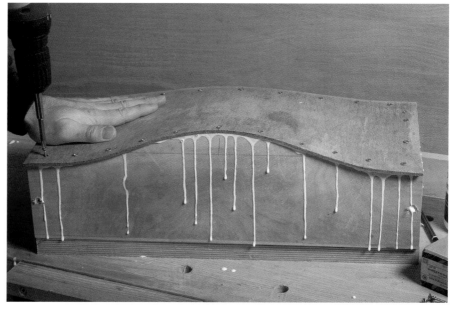

1 Making the formers: part 1
Use the grids on the drawings as a guide when plotting the curved shapes of the formers. Cut out the shapes on the bandsaw as accurately as possible and assemble with 50 mm (2 in) screws. Use the spokeshave and block plane to smooth and modify the edges, as shown above. Press a sheet of plywood against the former to see how well it fits and make adjustments as necessary.

2 Making the formers: part 2
With the two parts of the seat former and two parts of the back former complete, cover the faces with plywood. The plywood should overhang the sides all around. Use plenty of glue and 15 mm (¹⁹⁄₃₂ in) screws to fix them together. Clean off the excess glue and allow to dry. Retract the screws and fill the holes. Plane off the protruding edges and sand smooth.

3 Laminating
Fix scrap pieces of wood to the sides of one half of each former to help locate the other half and to stop the laminated wood from slipping. Apply varnish and wax polish to the formers. Practise laminating. Spread glue on the plywood to be laminated, place it in the former and force the two parts together with clamps.

4 Cutting the seat and back
Once the seat and back are dry, remove them from the formers and mark on the outlines of the finished shapes. Cut out on the bandsaw (ensure the curved workpiece has adequate contact with the worktable) as accurately as possible. Smooth and flatten the edges with a smoothing plane.

5 Shaping the seat rails

The shape of the seat rails must conform to the shape of the seat. Use the seat as a template for the seat rails: draw around it, and cut out the shape with the bandsaw. The back end of the rail requires an angled edge (canted – see step 6 photo); again, use the seat as a template to gauge the angle and the spokeshave and block plane to remove the waste.

6 Assembling the seat

Drill the pivot holes in the seat rails before fixing them to the seat. Use the combination bit to drill fixing holes through the seat and into the rails. Glue and screw together. Wipe off the excess glue. Plug the screwholes, allow to dry and shave off the ends of the plugs to produce a smooth finish.

7 Cutting the mortise and tenon joints

Mark out the positions of the mortise and tenon joints. Cut the mortises first and clean out the corners with the chisel. Cut the tenons on the sliding compound mitre saw. Check that they fit properly. Cut the shape on the front stretcher after completing the tenons. Smooth the curved edge with the spokeshave.

8 Completing the chair

Cut the slots in the long legs with the router, as shown above. Drill pivot holes in the short legs. Glue and clamp the leg frames, check that they are square and allow to dry. Sand all surfaces smooth and apply a varnish finish. Make the metal plates (or ask a metalworker to make them for you). Attach the plates and assemble the chair using the metal fixings.

GLOSSARY

Arris A corner or sharp edge where two surfaces meet.

Banding A narrow plain or patterned strip of veneer used to make a decorative feature.

Batten A narrow strip of wood, bigger than a beading but smaller than a plank or board.

Beading A thin strip of wood with a shaped profile.

Blank A piece of wood suitably sized for making a carving or turning.

Burl or **burr** A bulbous growth (usually on the trunk) of some species (walnut, for example). These sections of wood are highly prized by woodturners. Inside are tightly packed clusters of dormant buds (buds that failed to form branches), which have dark centres. Also used for making decorative veneers.

Butting Pushing one piece of wood hard up against another to obtain a good fit, or to achieve a joint.

Carcass The skeleton, framework or shell of a structure.

Centring Setting a measurement or component part on the centre of another, or measuring a length or width to find the centre.

Clamping up The procedure of assembling components with glue and applying pressure with clamps.

Compound mitre A cut that is angled (not 90°) in two planes. It can be achieved on a compound mitre saw by setting a "mitre" angle and a "tilt" angle.

Crosscutting Sawing or otherwise cutting across the run of the grain.

Dry run; to dry-assemble Putting all the parts together without glue, pins or screws to check that joints and structure work.

End grain Cross-section grain at the end of a piece of timber (a plank or board).

Face edge The first surface to be planed adjacent and at 90° to the face side.

Face side The first side to be planed; the flat surface from which all the other faces and sides are measured.

Fence An adjustable guide that is used to set the distance of a line of cut from an edge.

Figure The grain pattern (see grain).

Finishing The procedure of sanding, painting, staining and fitting hardware (wheels, catches, handles and hinges) to bring a project to a good conclusion.

Former A shape or corresponding shapes used to bend (mould) veneers to create permanently curved (laminated) components. A shape for moulding solid wood while steam bending.

Forstner bit A large-diameter bit used for drilling flat-bottomed holes.

Grain The appearance and texture of wood; wood fibres create unique texture, colour and pattern.

Hardwood Botanically speaking, hardwood comes from broadleafed, deciduous trees. It is usually harder than softwood but it is more a term to describe a wood's general characteristics.

Jig A home-made or shop-bought structure or device used to hold a workpiece or a tool in a fixed position, so that you can repeat the cutting, drilling or planing operation.

Laminating The act of gluing, pegging or otherwise joining several pieces of wood together.

Levelling Using a spirit-level to decide whether or not a structure or component part is horizontally or vertically level; then making adjustments to bring the component into line.

Marking out Using a pencil, ruler, square and compass to draw lines on a piece of wood in readiness for cutting.

Mock-up A rough construction used to test out a design. If you like a particular design but want to make changes to it, it is a good idea to make a mock-up to see if the changes will work.

Moulding A strip of wood with a decorative profile.

Offcuts Small pieces of wood that are left over after you have cut out the primary shapes or forms; these can often be used at a later date.

Planning The whole procedure of considering a project, looking at wood, making drawings, working out quantities, measurements and costs and so on, prior to actually starting the project.

Preserving Painting wood with a chemical in order to ensure that it is protected against mould and rot. Depending upon the project, the wood can be preserved before or after a finish has been applied, or the preservative can be a finish in its own right.

Profile A shape as seen from the side, a cross-section shape or a flat outline shape.

PVA glue White woodworking adhesive (a polyvinyl acetate), which is good for most woodworking applications.

Sanding Using a series of graded sandpapers on the surface of wood to achieve a smooth finish. This can be done at various stages during a project – a swift sanding after the wood has been shaped and jointed, another when assembled, and then a final one after a first coat of varnish.

Sighting Judging by eye, or by looking down a tool or down a length of wood, to determine whether a cut, joint or structure is level or true.

Squaring The technique of marking out, cutting and fixing wood so that surfaces or structures are at right angles (90°) to one another.

Waney edge The edge of a plank still retaining the irregular shape and bark from the outside of the tree.

SUPPLIERS

Your local general DIY store is likely to stock all the power tools used in this book. It may also stock useful sections of prepared softwood. For specialist hand tools and woodwork machinery, find a local tool and machine retailer or use a mail-order company. You will need to collect small quantities of rough-sawn timber and manufactured boards from your local timberyard. Some timberyards can prepare timber and boards to your specifications.

UNITED KINGDOM

Hardwood retailers and timberyards

North Heigham Sawmills Ltd
26 Paddock Street
Norwich
Norfolk
NR2 4TW
Tel: 01603 622978

South London Hardwoods
390 Sydenham Road
Croydon
Surrey
CR0 2EA
Tel: 020 8683 0292

Timbmet Group Ltd
PO Box 39
Cumnor Hill
Oxford
OX2 9PP
Tel: 01865 862223
www.timbmet.com

Veneer and inlay suppliers

Anita Marquetry Ltd
Unit 6–7 Dole Road
    Enterprise Park
Llandrindod Wells
Powys
LD1 6DF
Tel: 01597 825505
www.marquetry.co.uk

Capital Crispin Veneer
Unit 12 Bow Industrial Park
Carpenter's Road
London
E15 2DZ
Tel: 020 8525 0300

Ironmongery

Isaac Lord
185 Desborough Road
High Wycombe
Buckinghamshire
HP11 2QN
Tel: 01494 462121

Router tables and accessories

Trend Machinery & Cutting
    Tools Ltd
Unit 6 St Alban's Road
Odhams Trading Estate
Watford
Hertfordshire
WD24 7TR
Tel: 01923 221910/249911

Tool retailers

Axminster Power Tool Centre
Axminster
Devon
EX13 5PH
Tel: 0800 371822
www.axminster.co.uk

Screwfix Direct Ltd
Houndstone Business Park
Yeovil
BA22 8RT
Tel: 01935 414100
www.screwfix.com

The following woodworking magazines can also provide a national overview of woodworking retailers:

Furniture & Cabinet Making
The Guild of Master Craftsmen
166 High Street
Lewes
East Sussex
BN7 1XU
Tel: 01273 488 005
www.thegmcgroup.com

Practical Woodworking and
    The Woodworker
Berwick House
8–10 Knoll Rise
Orpington
Kent
BR6 0EL
Tel: 01689 899200
www.getwoodworking.com

Traditional Woodworking
The Well House
High Street
Burton-on-Trent
Staffordshire
DE14 1JQ
Tel: 01283 742950

SOUTH AFRICA

Timber retailers

Citiwood
339 Main Reef Road
Denver 2094 (Johannesburg)
Tel: 011 622 9360

Coleman Timbers
Unit 3, Willowfield Crescent
Springfield Park Industria 4091
    (Durban)
Tel: 031 579 1565

Federated Timbers
17 McKenzie Street
Industrial Sites
Bloemfontein 9301
Tel: 051 447 3171

Penny Pinchers
261 Lansdowne Road
Claremont 7780 (Cape Town)
Tel: 021 683 0380

Timber City
74 5th Avenue
Newton Park 6045 (Port
    Elizabeth)
Tel: 041 365 3586

Hardware and DIY retailers

Mica
(outlets nationwide)
Tel: 031 573 2442
www.mica.co.za

Wardkiss Paint and Hardware
    Centre
329 Sydney Road
Durban 4001
Tel: 031 205 1551

Tool retailers

J & J Sales
38 Argyle Street
East London 5201
Tel: 043 743 3380

Tooltrick
55A Bok Street
Pietersburg 0700
Tel: 015 295 5982

AUSTRALIA

General DIY stores

Carroll's Woodcraft Supplies
66 Murradoc Road
Drysdale
Vic 3222
Tel: 03 5251 3874
www.cws.au.com

Hardware

Boxmakers Brassware
PO Box 136 Dungog
NSW 2420
Tel 02 4992 3068
www.boxmakersbrassware.com.au

Mother of Pearl & Sons Trading
Rushcutters Bay
34–36 McLachlan Avenue
NSW 2011
Tel: 02 9332 4455

Timber suppliers

Aw Swadling Timber
    & Hardware Pty Ltd
92–94 Lilyfield Road
Rozelle
NSW 2039
Tel: 02 9810 4177
www.hntgordon.com.au

Trend Timbers
Lot 1
Cunneen Street
Mulgrave/McGrath's Hill
NSW 2756
Tel: 02 4577 5277
www.trendtimbers.com.au

Tool retailers

Carba-Tec Pty Ltd
(outlets nationwide)
Head Office:
40 Harries Road
Coorparoo
QLD 4151
Tel: 07 3397 2577
www.carbatec.com.au

Colen Clenton
20 Long Street
Cessnock 2325
Tel 02 4990 7956

Hare & Forbes Machinery
    House
(outlets nationwide)
Head Office:
The Junction
2 Windsor Road
Northmead
NSW 2152
Tel: 02 9890 9111
www.hareandforbes.com.au

H. N. T. Gordon & Co Classic
    Plane Makers
50 Northcott Crescent
Alstonville
NSW 2477
Tel: 612 6628 7222
www.hntgordon.com.au

Timbecon Pty Ltd
10–12 John Street
Bentley
WA 6102
Tel: 08 9356 1653
www.timbecon.com.au

The Wood Works Book
    & Tool Co
8 Railway Road
Meadowbank
NSW 2114
Tel 02 9807 7244
www.thewoodworks.com.au

NEW ZEALAND

General DIY stores

Bunnings Warehouse
(outlets nationwide)
www.bunnings.co.nz

Hammer Hardware
(outlets nationwide)
Private Bag 102925
North Shore Mail Centre
Auckland 1330
Tel: 09 443 9953
www.hammerhardware.co.nz

Mitre 10 (New Zealand) Ltd
(outlets nationwide)
Private Bag 102925
North Shore Mail Centre
Auckland
Tel: 09 443 9900
www.mitre10.co.nz

PlaceMakers
(outlets nationwide)
Support Office:
15- Marua Road
Ellerslie
Auckland
Tel: 09 525 5100
www.placemakers.co.nz

INDEX